Marjorie Rieu

André Rieu

My Music, My Life

Translated by Diane Webb

André Rieu: My Music, My Life
First published in 1996
Revised edition printed in the UK in 2014 by Hardie Grant Books

Hardie Grant Books (UK)
5th & 6th Floors
52–54 Southwark Street
London SE1 1UN
www.hardiegrant.co.uk

Hardie Grant Books (Australia)
Ground Floor, Building 1
658 Church Street
Melbourne, VIC 3121
www.hardiegrant.com.au

© Photos: Private Collection André & Marjorie Rieu; Wil Dekkers;
Fotopersbureau Dijkstra bv; Foto Harry Disch; Studiopress Guy van Grinsven;
André Rieu Productions BV; Foto Peter Schols; Jean-Jacques Spuisers.
Cover Photo © Govert de Roos
Back Cover Photo © Gregor Ramaekers

British Library Cataloguing-in-Publication Data. A catalogue record
for this book is available from the British Library.

ISBN 978 178488007 1
Translated by Diane Webb
Cover design: Ami Smithson
Colour Reproduction by p2d
Printed and bound by CPI Group (UK) Ltd,
Croydon, CR0 4YY

10 9 8 7 6 5 4 3 2 1

FOREWORD

*F*or my dear fans all over the world:

When I was small, only five years old, my mother gave me a violin. From that moment I had only one dream: when I grew up I wanted to go on stage and play to lots of people. I wanted to make everyone in the world happy with my music. I didn't care how long it took me to get there – I knew I would make it!

I'll never forget the year my dream came true: 1994. (Funnily enough, it's a bit like my year of birth, 1949.) After years of studying and working, I had a breakthrough with my recording of Shostakovich's *Second Waltz*, first in my home country of the Netherlands, then, in the following years, in the rest of Europe, North and South America, Australia, South Africa and Asia.

My fans all over the world have made that little boy's dream come true: the boy with his child-sized violin, who wanted to make the whole world happy with his music. I thank you all from the bottom of my heart.

Since that breakthrough in 1994, my orchestra and I have had a lot of attention from radio, television, newspapers and magazines. Everything we have done has been extensively documented in the media; wherever we go, we are filmed and photographed and written about. That's how it goes once you're well known. But what about all the years before then? All the years of my childhood growing up in our large family, my time at school, my time as a student at the academy of music, and the time when I was getting to know my wife Marjorie and setting out on a life together with her? In this book Marjorie has described all that for me.

My Music, My Life is the story of that little boy who dreamed of one day standing on the stage with his violin, until the moment when his big breakthrough came.

CONTENTS

INTRODUCTION

*T*his book was written for my fans, for all those people who love my music so much that they not only come to my concerts, but also write to me again and again to say how much they enjoy them. Every day I receive letters from all over the world, from fans who tell me that my music means so much to them, that it cheers them up and helps them get through hard times, that sometimes it even seems to possess healing qualities – in short, that my music makes them happy.

Although lack of time prevents me from reading all these letters myself, I'm told the essence of the messages they contain, and I think it's fantastic that people confide all this to me. They don't have to worry that their letters won't be read or perhaps won't even arrive, because by now the postman knows exactly where I live. Letters with the barest trace of an address – 'André Rieu, on the Maas', 'Violinist in Limburg',[1] even letters with only my photograph on the envelope – are delivered safe and sound to my office. And time and again it does me good to hear the enthusiastic stories they contain, urging me and my musicians to carry on with what we're doing – making music and bringing pleasure to people – and to take our task seriously.

Naturally it's impossible for me to answer all my fan mail. First of all (and this is something I probably have in common with lots of men), I hate to write letters. When I was young my parents always complained that, unlike my prolific sisters, I never wrote home when I was on holiday. In general, women seem to get a lot more pleasure out of writing letters, even incredibly long ones, which is one reason my wife Marjorie was kind enough to offer to write my life story for me. My other excuse is that if I had to answer all my fan mail I would never have any time left over to practice the violin, and that is probably the last thing my fans would want.

For these reasons I've decided to answer all these wonderful letters

---

[1] Limburg is the southernmost province of the Netherlands.

in the form of a book, in which I'll attempt to answer the many questions posed by my fans, young and old, and also to make clear that success isn't something that just falls into your lap like manna from heaven. I hope this will be some consolation to young people of all professions who feel as though they do nothing but slave away and never actually achieve anything. If you keep at it long enough (for about forty years!), never give up, and – perhaps the most important thing – always enjoy what you're doing, then sooner or later you're bound to succeed!

For years I've received fan mail from all parts of the English-speaking world, so I'm especially pleased that this book has now been translated into English. But no matter where my fans come from and no matter which language they speak, I would like to say this to all of them: Marjorie and I have taken great pleasure in writing this book for all those people interested in learning more about me and how I got started, and for everyone whose daily lives are made a little bit happier by my music.

My Work /
My (Private) Life

*F*or the past thirty-five years my private life has been so inextricably tied up with my work that it all blends together into one and the same story, especially because Marjorie, from the very beginning, has always been closely involved with my work. My current success is due to the energy that both of us have invested all these years in my career. The two of us have built a life together that includes not only our family but also our business, which is responsible for managing my two orchestras, The Maastricht Salon Orchestra and The Johann Strauss Orchestra. So it is no wonder that all this work fills up a good deal of our private life, often making it difficult to say where one ends and the other begins. We both love our work, and that is a great incentive – especially when its success is so evident – to carry on with it and to put all the energy we have into making it succeed. Our life is music, pure and simple. It occupies our every moment, though it never gets to be a burden. (We occasionally get fed up, however, with the burdensome tasks that such a business inevitably entails!)

Even when we go for walks or when we're on holiday, we often talk about music, thinking up ideas for new programs or new texts, or discussing – without really meaning to – ideas for the new concert season. There are times, of course, when we – or our children! – have enough of it, and then we're quite capable of turning our attention to something else, though I must confess this is never for long.

In addition to the story of my youth and student years, this book contains mainly facts and anecdotes from my musical career: the interesting, remarkable, nice and not-so-nice things that I've experienced on the long road leading to my present success.

These events have naturally taken up a large part of my private life, so I've described in detail what I felt as they were happening – the emotions accompanying my success story. Doubts, fears, stress, and disappointments – these feelings are all unavoidable, but they must be overcome if you want to reach your goal, no matter what your profession.

On the other hand, happiness, excitement, and enthusiasm give you the strength to go on with your work, until at last you succeed.

I don't want to give the impression, though, that I'm obsessed with my work, or that I'm under such stress that I can't stop for a moment to enjoy life. On the contrary, we usually work in a very relaxed atmosphere and really love what we're doing. In fact, I can scarcely imagine a more agreeable private life!

CHRONOLOGY

*M*y life story is more like a mosaic, a self-portrait composed of fragmentary images, than like a real autobiography, so I have set down the basic facts of my life in outline form, in order to make the rest of the book easier to read.

(N.B.: I was never very good at remembering dates, so some of these are only approximations.)

1949   My father and very pregnant mother move from Amsterdam to Maastricht. I am born a few days later, thereby just barely qualifying as a 'Maastrichtenaar'. At birth I already have two sisters and later acquire two brothers and another sister.

1954   My first violin lessons.
1954–1960   Elementary school; violin lessons continue.
1961–1967   High school, with the emphasis on scientific subjects and both modern and classical languages; violin lessons continue.
1962   I Meet Marjorie for the first time.
1968–1973   Conservatory of music in both Maastricht and Liège (Belgium); violin lessons from, among others, Jo Juda and Herman Krebbers (both concertmasters of Amsterdam's Concertgebouw Orchestra).
1974   I renew acquaintance with Marjorie.
1974–1977   Brussels Conservatory; violin lessons from André Gertler.
1975   Marriage to Marjorie.
1977   Final examinations (Premièr Prix) at the Brussels Conservatory.

1978	Birth of our son Marc; The Maastricht Salon Orchestra is founded.
1978–1989	Member of The Limburg Symphony Orchestra.
1978–1996	The Maastricht Salon Orchestra plays in the Netherlands, Belgium, Germany, and the United States.
1981	Birth of our son Pierre.
1987	The Johann Strauss Orchestra and our own business, André Rieu Productions, are founded.
1988–1996	The Johann Strauss Orchestra tours the Netherlands, Belgium, and Germany with a program of Viennese music.
1992	Death of my father, André Rieu Sr.
1994	Release and success of *The Second Waltz* and *Strauss & Co. (From Holland With Love)*; the Netherlands falls under the spell of the waltz.
1995	In the Top Ten the whole year; solo performance during half-time of Ajax's (Amsterdam's soccer team) Champions League match for a capacity crowd of 60,000; *Wiener Mélange (The Vienna I Love)* enters the charts as Number One of the Top 100. Seven times platinum for *From Holland With Love*.
1996	I receive the World Music Award. Starting in 1996 and continuing to the present day, I take The Johann Strauss Orchestra touring all over the world.
2000	I build the André Rieu Studios where we always rehearse and record a CD every year. We go to the most beautiful locations for the concerts you can see on our DVDs – including *Romantic Paradise* in Cortona (Tuscany), Radio City Music Hall in New York, Michaelerplatz in Vienna, the Flower Island of Mainau, the Semper Opera in Dresden, Heidelberg, the Belvedere Palace in Vienna and the fairy tail park Efteling, the setting of one of our most beautiful DVDs *Wonderland*. Last but not least, our own castle in Maastricht provides the decor for the super-romantic DVD *Home for Christmas*.
2006	We perform in Vienna in front of the Schönbrunn Palace, which gives me the idea of building a replica of the palace and taking it with us all over the world in 120 containers. Doing this brings us worldwide renown, and on the other hand nearly brings financial ruin to our business. I promise Marjorie solemnly never to take financial risks like this again! Since 2005 we play every summer on the Vrijthof Square in Maastricht, my hometown and the place of my birth. Fans come from all over the world to be at the concert, and year after year it's such a fantastic occasion.

2010	Performance in the Royal Variety Show in the presence of Queen Elizabeth.
2011	Sir Anthony Hopkins sends me a wonderful, melancholy waltz of his own composition, with the request to record it with my orchestra. I feel so honoured and happy. In Vienna the world premiere of this waltz takes place in the presence of Sir Anthony himself, who is moved to tears. His waltz, entitled *The Waltz Goes On* appears on our CD and DVD of the same name.
2013	We have the honour of being invited to give a huge open-air concert in Amsterdam to mark the coronation of King Willem Alexander and Queen Máxima. In the UK I get my own TV series: *Welcome to My World*.
2014	For the tenth year in a row we give our traditional Vrijthof concert in Maastricht, this time with a Venetian flavour. In the autumn the CD and DVD *Love in Venice* appear.

PART ONE

BOYHOOD DREAMS

I wouldn't recognise myself,
but insiders say it's really me.

ANGELS
AND THE
SOUND OF VIOLINS

*W*omen have always played an important role in my life. My first true love was the principal of the kindergarten I attended, the very reverend and also very dear Sister Clara Magdala. She was a real angel and used to lead me, a chubby little toddler, by the hand across the playground. Going on walks with her was pure bliss. Together we looked at the tall trees and the other children, and at birds that surprised me by being able to hang onto walls. This woman apparently made such a deep impression on me that all other memories of my early childhood pale into insignificance next to my memory of her. Of those first years of my life – the only period I spent without the violin – I can recall only one image: a playground with tall chestnut trees, little birds hanging from the wall, and that wonderful, beloved nun, who took me by the hand and guided me on my first steps in the outside world.

Not long afterwards the violin entered my life, and with 'her', (naturally 'violin' is a feminine noun in Dutch!) a beautiful, young violin teacher with blue eyes and gorgeous, curly blonde hair – 'golden hair', I used to call it. And once again, in spite of my tender age of five, I was head-over-heels in love. My mother told me that once in a while she would peek in while I was having a lesson and would see me, entranced, staring at Miss Christina with eyes wide open and mouth agape, letting my violin and bow dangle carelessly against my knee.

It wasn't just her gorgeous curls that filled me with admiration, though. Right from the start I was overawed at the wonderful way she let her left hand tremble super-fast, while her fingers made only the slightest movement on the strings of her violin. Mastering the art of vibrato, which is the proper term for it, is essential for producing a beautiful sound and for playing expressively.

I wanted to be able to do that too, that I was sure of! And although I could still barely play the violin, I practiced and practiced, until I felt that I had also mastered the art. It was a terrific feeling, finally being able to play with vibrato. I remember how proud I was, conjuring up such a beautiful sound with my violin. From that moment on I knew that when I grew up I wanted to be a violinist.

This desire became even stronger when I was allowed for the first time to go with my father, conductor of The Limburg Symphony Orchestra, to one of his concerts. Breathlessly I watched the gestures he made in front of what to the eyes of a child seemed an immense orchestra. Filled with awe, I watched that enormous group of string players, especially the violins with all those bows going up and down at the same time. A fascinating picture, one I'll never forget as long as I live, just like that unforgettable, full sound of the strings, which I still find the most beautiful and romantic sound that exists.

After that concert I dreamed of standing on stage and playing beautiful music for lots and lots of people. First, of course, I would have to practice hard, day in and day out, week after week and year after year. Not only did I have violin lessons twice a week – at first from the angelic Miss Christina and later on from very exacting teachers – but I also had to practice every day. Needless to say, this was something I didn't always feel like doing. After school, when all the other children were playing outside, I first had to practice the violin for an hour, something my mother was very strict about. I liked best to take my violin and stand in front of the window, dreamily improvising melodies. But was I ever in trouble if my mother caught me doing it!

My first (much too large!) violin.

'Practice!' she would immediately yell from downstairs. And it was good that she did, because without scales and technical studies you'll never learn to play the violin. I could see this myself, of course, so back I went to practicing my études.

The older I got, though, the easier it became for me to keep my mind on my studies.

Several years ago I heard the Russian cellist Rostropovich say in an interview on television that as a child he had taped himself playing scales. He would then play the tape in his room, with the volume turned up really loud so that his mother was sure to hear it, and go merrily outside to play. I've known Rostropovich since I was a boy, and I've never forgotten that he always had a lively imagination! I doubt whether the tape recorder had even been invented when he was a child, but if I'd known of such a trick when I was small, I would have made use of it gladly.

From top to bottom: my father, my sisters Cilia and Teresia, myself, and my brother Robert.

As the children of a conductor we were naturally given a solid grounding in music. This meant a lot more than just having violin lessons. Before long I was also having piano and recorder lessons, and later I even played the oboe for a while. Once, when I was in high school, I played for the famous Dutch recorder player Frans Brüggen, who thought I had some talent and saw to it that I was given proper lessons. These were only to be had in Eindhoven, so every week I had to spend an hour each way on the train, going to my recorder lesson – no small task for a boy who already had his hands full with school, the violin, and

21

teenage infatuations.

Of all the instruments the violin was my favourite, so I studied diligently and never missed the opportunity to hear a famous violinist playing a concerto with my father's symphony orchestra. After the concert they would often come to our house, and each and every one of them was an important influence on me. The famous violinists I saw and heard included Herman Krebbers and Theo Olof (at that time the two concertmasters of Amsterdam's Concertgebouw Orchestra), Yehudi Menuhin, Arthur Grumiaux, Leonid Kogan, and David Oistrach. Krebbers performed almost every year with my father. I admired him even more than the others, not only because of his virtuosity, but also because of his tremendous charisma. I'm still proud of the fact that I had lessons from him. As a small boy I already wanted to become just as famous as he was, and in my dreams I stood on stage in the spotlights, playing for a full house.

What probably influenced my career as a musician more than anything else is the fact that for years I sang in a church choir. Besides the lessons on various instruments and the weekly trip to the concert hall to see my father conduct, the choir was an integral part of my musical education. Every Wednesday and Saturday afternoon my younger brother Robert and I went to sing in the St Servatius choir, conducted by Benoit Franssen. We called it, rather irreverently, 'that old man's choir'. We never felt like going. Whenever it was time for us to go to choir practice, the boys in our neighbourhood would be playing football or doing something else that looked like fun. How often the two of us cursed that choir! To make matters worse, during the hour before choir practice we had solfège lessons from 'the old man', who taught according to a dreaded Belgian method.[2] Every week we would think up another excuse to get out of going to solfège lessons and choir practice. If we weren't sick to our stomachs or ill in some other way, then we said we'd lost our exercise books or our shoes, or we simply ran off and hid someplace where our mother couldn't find us. Once we even officially excused ourselves and our friend Jérôme, on behalf of our parents, to the conductor, but our strategy backfired, and we were forced to go back to choir practice with our heads bowed in disgrace. My parents, who weren't so strict in other respects, were implacable where music was concerned. And we were lucky they were, because looking back on it 'the old man' wasn't all that bad, and we benefited greatly from his strict lessons. (Incidentally, our friend Jérôme's parents also forced him to stay in the choir and stick to

---

[2] Solfège is the practice of solmization, or singing music to the syllables do-re-mi, etc.

his solfège lessons. He is now a well-known recorder player, teaches at the conservatory of music, and leads a Baroque ensemble.)

The crazy thing was that we quite enjoyed it, once we were finally there rehearsing with the choir. Besides, we were as pleased as punch to sing at high mass on Sunday mornings and at vespers on Sunday afternoons. For that matter, I gradually began to discover that there were quite a few nice girls in the choir, and I fell in love with them by turns. By this time I no longer minded singing in the choir at all.

After you'd been a member of the choir for a while you were allowed to walk in the yearly St Servatius procession. What a treat that was!

After high mass the procession assembled in the sun-flooded cloister garden of the St Servatius Church, where you could see all those splendidly dressed people, hundreds of them, shuffling into place in line. Some were dressed as light-blue angels with real wings and some as brides in white, waving palm branches, while the priests in gold-brocade chasubles marched along under a magnificent canopy. Memories never to be

With my sisters Teresia (left) and Cilia (right) in the neighbourhood where I grew up.

forgotten! Especially the moment when the singing began, accompanied by a brass band, and the procession started to move forward slowly. Then a shiver went down your spine from the thrill of beholding such a beautiful sight. When I was a bit older I belonged to the group in the choir that got to swing the thurible, or censer, while singing and marching solemnly in the procession in a special, halting way, taking a step and then slowly dragging your other foot forward and tapping your toe before taking the next step. This was just about the pinnacle of a choirboy's career. (Later on in this book my brother Robert tells of my bungling beginnings as a censer swinger.)

The high point of the choir's year was without a doubt Christmas. You looked forward to it the whole year long, because, when it came right down to it, this was what it was all about. At Christmas all those hours of practice finally paid off, because then the church was full to overflowing with an 'audience'.

It began with the singing of evening mass, or vespers, followed by three masses in a row. After the last one – midnight mass – we went home to eat *stollen*, the traditional fruit cake made at Christmas time, and go to bed. The next day we were again present at high mass in the morning and at vespers in the afternoon. It seems like hard work, but for a choirboy it was the crowning glory of a year's practice.

The midnight mass made the deepest impression on Robert and me. There you stood with the whole choir, dressed in a red robe and white surplice, high up in the choir loft. From this vantage point you could see the whole church, breathe in the penetrating smell of incense as it wafted up from below, and gaze down upon the crowd of worshippers, who turned around after the mass to face the choir and sing Christmas carols with us. When it was over they even clapped for the choir – the only time of the year when there was applause in the church. And then you were as happy as can be, and you forgot all those Wednesday and Saturday afternoons when you weren't allowed to play with your friends.

I'm convinced that the foundation of my romantic approach
to music was laid then and there, during those processions
and midnight masses at Christmas. The magnificently decorated
church, full to overflowing, the nativity scene with its beautiful statues
and angels hovering above it; Corelli's moving Christmas music,
and the smell of flowers and incense: it all fell into place and was part
of a unique and impressive event, which, if you ask me, had a lot
more to do with theatre than with religion.

VIOLIN MUSIC?
CONSTANT DRILLING!

'How wonderful it must be to make your hobby your profession!' I can't tell you how often I've heard people say this, especially those who put their heart and soul into playing an instrument simply as a hobby, as a way to wind down and relax after work. It should be obvious by now, though, that music for me as a child was anything but relaxing. Violin, recorder, and solfège lessons, church choir, concerts – in our family all this was part of the daily routine, the same as going to school, or washing your hands and praying before meals. It was all compulsory and there was no getting out of it. Even though I dreamed of becoming a famous violinist 'when I grew up', that didn't mean I wanted to think about nothing but music the whole day long. On the contrary! Just like other children, I had a natural aversion to anything I was forced to do, and besides, there were a lot of things that interested me much more than music.

To begin with, there was that construction on wheels that my brother Robert and I designed. It was an outstanding example of technical ingenuity, which served in our neighbourhood as a vehicle of public transportation for younger brothers and sisters, friends, dogs, rabbits, and other household pets. Members of our family and also our neighbours referred to this vehicle respectfully as 'the Cart'.

The Cart took over our lives; Robert and I devoted every spare minute to it. Our minds were constantly occupied with ways to smarten up our much-loved brainchild and bring it to technical perfection. Every rusted screw, twisted wire, warped board – in other words, everything that unimaginative grown-ups considered worthless and threw away – we managed to find some use for. 'We could use it for the Cart!' is still a much-used expression in my family and a euphamism for 'useless junk'.

Originally a sort of pushcart – no more than the metal frame of an old baby carriage with a plank on top – the Cart gradually grew into an improvised 'semi' with attached trailer, complete with steering mechanism. It was actually the forerunner of the 'Straussmobile'.[3] I was completely obsessed with that thing! Often at school, during a particularly boring lesson, inspiration would strike and I'd suddenly realise how we could attach an old steering wheel we'd found somewhere to the Cart. And then my legs couldn't carry me home fast enough to put my idea into practice.

And homework? Oh, well, there would always be time for that later. I must confess that I was very good at putting things off. In the course of my school career I developed a rather accurate method of calculating the possibility of being given a test. My system worked so well that in the end it was at least partly responsible for my continuing school at gymnasium (university entrance) level, though this unfortunately reflects little credit on my teachers.

[3] This is the name given by The Johann Strauss Orchestra to the luxurious bus in which it has travelled to concerts for the past few years.

A drawing I made in 1964: a church in Caramagna (northern Italy).

The technical possibilities of the Cart – its driving and steering mechanisms, that kind of thing – were a source of endless fascination for me as a boy. But I was interested not just in the technical aspects of building, say, a car. What filled me with awe more than anything, especially when I was a bit older, was the construction of new houses. If there was anything being built in the neighbourhood, I invariably went there to watch, trying to take in the skills displayed by the construction workers. I learned absolutely everything this way, from excavating a foundation – a hole in a pristine meadow, the most impressive thing by far – to putting the finishing touches onto a bathroom. Every detail was interesting and provided a worthwhile lesson. As soon as a worker entered our house – to lay a new parquet floor, say, or to repair something – I was there in a flash to watch and offer my help, which is how I learned about the handiwork of carpenters, masons, plumbers, electricians, and roofers. Building and technology were my greatest hobbies. I made cupboards and built sheds; constructed brick walls; installed romantic, indirect lighting in the attic; soldered taps; and repaired refrigerators and washing machines. Later on I even built a whole bathroom onto a country house, including connecting it to the well, re-laying the sewage pipes, and wiring it for electricity. Unfortunately all of my construction projects had one big disadvantage: I insisted they be strong enough to withstand any storm, even one of hurricane proportions, and preferably even earthquakes. All of my constructions were built of such sturdy materials and with such attention to detail that a demolition crew would have had to be called in to knock them down again.

No one was surprised when I eventually voiced my desire to become an architect, since I not only liked to build things but was also an enthusiastic draftsman, specialising in houses, churches, and landscapes. For years I drew passionately, anywhere I happened to be, whether at home in Maastricht or on holiday in the south of France or Italy, where the landscape and architecture held such charms for me that I never tired of filling page after page with sketches.

Why all these passions – because that is really the only way to describe them – finally gave way to the violin, I really don't know. Perhaps that childhood dream of mine, those first impressions I had of the excitement of concerts and the desire to play for an audience, was so strong that nothing could compete with it. I guess I was just destined to become a violinist. All my other interests were, and continue to be, just hobbies. I'm still fascinated by technology and building houses, although nowadays this interest is expressed in different ways than it used to be. I now put the skills I acquired in this field to good use in my business, so that I can oversee all the technical aspects and never have to feel as though I'm at the mercy of the 'experts.' One thing I have given up for good is using utility knives (the kind with razor-sharp blades) and circular saws, to the great relief, incidentally, of the company that insures my hands!

LET THERE BE LIGHT
(AND NO SMOKE PLEASE!)

*M*y brother Robert and I were inseparable as children. He was, and still is, a big clown, always capable of making me laugh so hard that I cry. He now lives in the south of France, in Marseilles, and unfortunately we hardly ever get to see each other. Robert recently sent me a story recalling our happy childhood years. It is exaggerated in the extreme, as are all his stories, but I feel I must share it with my readers anyway.

'I still have no idea what on earth induced us (by us I mean my younger brother Jean-Philippe, who was ten years old at the time, and myself) to ask André to take part in the evening prayer service, or vespers, in the great Basilica in Maastricht. Vespers was supposed to start at five o'clock, but traditionally began at ten past five.

Jean-Philippe and I were experienced altar boys, whereas André had never learned the art. He didn't even know, for example, when you were supposed to swing the censer, which brings us to the heart of the matter: André only came along that day on the condition that he be allowed to do exactly that – swing the censer. He promised to follow all of our instructions to the letter; so that none of the worshippers would notice that one of the altar boys was thoroughly unschooled. At first things went smoothly enough, and André managed to do almost everything we'd agreed upon without mishap.

He waited impatiently until at last the sacred moment arrived, the sacred moment being when the chosen one has to go over to the main altar and start warming up the censer. You have to keep the fire burning by making small waving movements with your hands so that when the time comes it produces just the right amount of smoke. In the space of one service an experienced altar boy can create a smoke screen of such impressive proportions that afterwards the sacristan needs a fog lamp to go and lock up the church.

André, therefore, took up his position and waited, slowly smouldering, for a curt nod from Jean-Philippe, which was the signal to start swinging the censer. We watched him skeptically out of the corner of our eye but were soon con-

vinced that we had an extremely professional censer-swinger in our midst. We consequently turned to our own duties and let André get on with his swinging.

It seemed as though every last bit of incense had to be used up. The censer turned faster and faster, and soon the sunlight falling through the windows was forced to make way for a dense, suffocating fog of the kind seen in highly industrialised areas or mining districts.

Up to this point we had found nothing surprising in the proceedings. André never does anything by halves, and, sure enough, the other half was yet to come.

The situation in the church was now such that the common prayer had turned into a massive chorus of throat-clearing and coughing. This was true only of those still breathing however, who were giving each other little slaps on the back. The others were being resuscitated in the side chapels by worshippers who had been trained in first aid. In the meantime, poor visibility had caused the priest to have the emergency lights turned on. At this point André tried to get our attention with a rather vulgar 'psst', a form of communication that's quite unusual in churches.

Meanwhile André's censer was still picking up speed. He continued to hiss 'psst' until we both finally turned our heads to look at him. We were just in time to see how his censer, which until now had only been swinging from left to right – though admittedly higher and higher – finally described a complete circle. It came down with a whoosh, and André immediately launched it into another orbit, swinging it powerfully around a second time, and a third, until it seemed that it would never stop.

By now André had planted his legs wide apart, probably to keep his balance. He looked more like a pitcher steadying himself before the wind-up than an altar boy.

Jean-Philippe and I had understood by this time that the situation had gotten completely out of hand. No one was in control anymore. Even the priest, suffering from lack of oxygen, had given up and was now feeling his way along the wall, making for home. Only André was beaming in the midst of his smoking merry-go-round, which had meanwhile begun to resemble a hand-driven propeller. The worst, though, was yet to come.

Either his muscles had begun to ache or he had had enough of it by this time. At any rate, André had decided to end the flight and come slowly down to earth. This was the risk you took with untrained altar boys, however, because now everything went completely wrong and a catastrophe could no longer be averted. You couldn't stop the 'ventilator' without mishap. No one could have, but nevertheless André wanted to stop, losing control of the steering for a moment. Instead of bringing the censer to an elegant stop with a virtuosic flourish, he slammed that antique silver object, dating from the fifteenth century, onto the floor at top speed. The glowing incense lay beside it, and the censer itself was transformed into an antique dent of unknown value. Thus André's clerical career came to an untimely end.

We turned our backs on that smoking heap of scrap metal and made our way home. No one said a word.

All of these valuable objects are now preserved in the Basilica's treasury. You can even make an appointment to go look at them. If you should see seven silver censers hanging there, one of which is nothing but one big dent, it has nothing to do with the Iconoclastic Fury.[4] It is simply that poor censer, which André Rieu was in the midst of swinging when it flew out of control and crashed to the floor one fateful day during vespers, the evening prayer service that was supposed to start at five o'clock but always started at ten past five.

Robert Rieu
Marseilles 1996

---

[4] In the Netherlands at the time of the Reformation (1566), public worship of the Catholic faith was banned, and many Catholic churches were stormed and images destroyed.

ALL YOU NEED
IS LOVE

*I*n the years following my childhood, from about the age of fourteen onward, there were actually only two things in my life: study and practice, practice and study! I can hardly remember doing anything else. School, violin ... violin, school ... it was all just a treadmill that never stopped. It wasn't so bad as long as things were going well, but there were times when nothing turned out right and then life was all misery and despair.

It was no wonder, then, that I fell in love at predictably regular intervals, taking refuge in my daydreams. When I found music theory boring, or had to wrestle with difficult physics problems, it was wonderful to become absorbed in my reveries about all kinds of pretty girls from school or the church choir. At the time it never amounted to anything more than fantasy, though, because school studies and the violin didn't leave me any time to put my wild dreams into practice.

Actually it wasn't so much a question of time. In our large family everyone played at least one instrument, so that at all times of the day there were scales and studies resounding from several rooms at once. You could hear a whole range of instruments: piano, recorder, trumpet, oboe, cello, violin, and harp. At the head of this mini-conservatory was our father-conductor.

It goes without saying that in a home where a conductor reigns, the study of music is taken very seriously indeed. Music was the centre of our lives; everything else had to give way to it. Things like going out with girls, just hanging around, or going out with friends for a beer – these were all taboo in our family. Instead, our life was filled with practicing études and sonatas and going to concerts of classical music. The Swinging Sixties quietly passed us by; I didn't even discover the existence of the Beatles and the Rolling Stones until they were making their comeback!

Although I find the Beatles' music especially good, I don't have the feeling that I was missing something at the time. The world consisted of Bach and Mozart, Stravinsky and Orff – we simply didn't know any better. Orff, especially, was a favourite among us children. In the hall next to the bathroom was a record player with 'the record of the month' on it, which was our own 'number one top hit'. For a long time it was Carl Orff's *Carmina Burana*. Before taking a bath we put it on so loud you could hear it with your head under water. It was wonderful! Mozart's opera *Così fan tutte* was also one of our 'bathroom hits' at one time. After a while we all knew it by heart, just like *Carmina Burana*, and could sing along with it in chorus.

For us, *Yesterday* didn't come along till 'the day after tomorrow'...

SAD
AND
LONELY

*A*fter high school Robert and I both studied for a few years at the conservatories in Maastricht and Liège. Liège is just over the border in the French-speaking part of Belgium, only half an hour from Maastricht, so we used to drive back and forth – both of us on one motor scooter – so that we could go on living at home.

I also made several study trips, to Germany, North and South America, and other places. In Germany I had become acquainted with the famous Hungarian violin teacher André Gertler, who was a professor at the Brussels Conservatory of Music. I now decided, at the age of twenty-four, to continue my studies with this teacher, and after passing a difficult audition I was admitted to his class.

I packed my things and went to Brussels, where I moved into a simple student apartment. This is a rather euphemistic term for a squalid hovel in the fifth-floor attic of an old, dilapidated house near the conservatory. The street I lived on could more or less be compared to the notorious 'Walletjes' in Amsterdam's red-light district. Much of what took place outside I couldn't see, however, because my garret had only one tiny window and the only thing you could see out of it was a bit of sky. The only nasty thing I ever laid eyes on was the weather, and the only really dangerous thing was perhaps the pungent smell of gas that hung in the air in that house. But my Bohemian accommodation had the great advantage of being cheap. After all, I had to get by on a meager student budget in the expensive city of Brussels.

It didn't work out as well as I had hoped, so off I went in search of work to earn myself a few extra francs. As luck would have it I happened upon a small, dark photographic studio where I was able to start work right away as a model. I was promised huge sums of money for ice skating in designer jeans or chewing cheerfully on a well-known piece of sugarless gum. The ideal job! I felt rich as a king and had supposedly already earned enough to cast my financial cares to the wind, for the first semester at least. Apparently I hadn't yet developed any business sense, though, because unfortunately I'd neglected to make arrangements that were legally binding. The studio proved to be good at photography, but not so good at paying its models. They were willing to pay me only if I would agree to pose in the nude. Ugh! I regretted having worked all those hours for nothing, but decided to renounce my claims for back pay. If it came to that, I'd rather be poor.

André Gertler was a very special person and I usually got along with him quite well. His fame as a teacher brought him pupils from all over the world; there were more than twenty nationalities in his class at that time. In addition to his extraordinary gifts as a teacher, he owed his fame to other things as well, including a talent for blustering around the class like a loose cannon. If he was in one of his black moods and decided that he didn't like your violin playing, there was a good chance he'd launch into a tirade, heaping abuse on you and not stopping till he'd torn you to pieces. Once he tore into a girl who'd just arrived from

The class of my violin teacher, André Gertler (front row, middle). I'm at the back, second from the left.

Argentina and was taking part for the first time in a class lesson. He went on for so long about one note that was out of tune that she finally lost her composure and ran out of the class in tears. She took the first flight to Buenos Aires and never returned.

If you really went too far and not only played a note out of tune, but also played it too loud or too soft, it sometimes happened that Monsieur Gertler positively exploded: to begin with, he would play the right note on the piano at least ten times – so hard that you were afraid he'd break the instrument – screaming at the same time 'ta, ta, ta, ta, ta....' He would then start panting so hard that his face turned red and blue, begin gasping for air, put on dark glasses and start searching desperately for his heart medicine. Finally, he would throw you out of the class, calling after you as you fled down the corridor that you should 'go and get a job at the music school in Timbuktu!' If you appeared in class again the next day and you'd practiced well, then he was friendliness itself, a truly amiable old gentleman who insisted you'd go far as a violinist!

The first time you witnessed one of his explosions you were scared to death, but after a while you realised that he only put on this act to get you to practice harder. Unbelievable! Besides, it was obvious that he really was an outstanding teacher. I learned a lot from him, at any rate, and that was the important thing.

All in all, my life as a student in that big city where I hardly knew a soul was, to tell the truth, a big disappointment. I had no friends whatsoever, especially at the beginning. The course was taxing, with all the compulsory subjects you had to take, and Gertler was demanding, so much so that everyone in our class did little else but practice. You didn't spend any time outside class getting to know our fellow students better. My brother Robert, the constant companion of my childhood years, was far away. He had become the lonely occupant of a similar garret in Vienna, where he studied the cello. I didn't have enough money to go out and have fun, and those violin lessons didn't do much to cheer me up either. My job had fallen through, the stuffy garret without a view didn't offer much inspiration, and there were no pretty girls to dream about in my limited circle of acquaintances. For the first time in my life I was lonely and extremely unhappy.

Here, shortly before my twenty-fifth birthday, the story of my youth and student years comes to an end. Luckily, only a few months later, my life took a turn for the better.

HAPPINESS!

*I*t must have been my lucky day, that day I went to visit Marjorie for the first time, thirty-eight years ago. I had been staying with an aunt of mine in Hilversum for a week, and had gone to the station to buy a one-way ticket to Maastricht. At least, that was my intention, but after I'd scraped together all the change from my coat and vest pockets and spread it out in front of the ticket-office window, it turned out not to be enough to take me all the way to my brand-new sweetheart.

Hmm... Now what? I looked questioningly at the girl behind the window. She drummed with her fingers on the counter and threw a meaningful glance over my shoulder at the people who were beginning to line up behind me.

I thought it over for a moment. Oh well, I said to myself, I'll just have to buy a ticket for as near as I can get. 'How far can I get on this much?' I asked the girl, who was becoming impatient.

'Just a minute,' she said, and her adding machine began ticking. 'Eindhoven,' she replied with cool calculation, not realising when she answered that the turn my life would take and my future career were hanging in the balance.

Apparently the gentleman standing behind me in line had more feeling for the tragedy of the situation. Maybe he'd noticed me because of the enormous fur hat I was wearing, the kind with ear flaps you can pull down and fasten with cords under your chin. Or maybe it was the violin case I was always carrying that had drawn his attention to me. I really don't know. In any case he tapped me on the shoulder, smiled, and asked in a friendly voice, 'Where would you like to go?'

'To my girlfriend in Maastricht,' I answered, surprised.

'May I offer to pay for the rest of your trip?'

I didn't know the man at all, but his face inspired such confidence that I completely disregarded the strict command I'd heard so often as a child – 'Never accept gifts from strangers!' – and gladly accepted his offer. I gratefully took the ticket for the whole trip from Hilversum to Maastricht and ran to the train, which I managed to catch just in time.

What luck, in fact, that that wide red plastic strip on the ground – the line that is supposed to guarantee your privacy nowadays in banks and airports – hadn't been invented yet. Because in that case I'm afraid that my life would have taken a very different turn, and not at all for the better.

Now that fate had driven me into the arms of Marjorie, who was waiting for me exactly at the appointed time on the platform in Maastricht, I was convinced that our being together would bring me happiness.

Unfortunately, I've never been able to find out who that nice gentleman was, whose generous gesture laid the foundation of my current success and happiness in life. I think if I were to see him again I would recognise him immediately. Who knows, he might even read this and remember the incident. (In that case, please get in touch with me, I still owe you a train ticket!)

That time I travelled from Hilversum to Maastricht alone. The trip took two hours, which seemed like an eternity. Marjorie and I made the return trip together, and it took twenty years! It was an exciting, sometimes difficult, but mostly pleasurable trip which seemed to fly by because we were together. After twenty years I was back again in Hilversum, *the* Hilversum this time, the home of Dutch radio and television broadcasting and therefore the Mecca of every Dutch artist.

All the success I now enjoy I owe to our having fought for it together. It wasn't always a conscious effort, of course, not as if we'd said, 'we'll put our shoulder to the wheel and in twenty years we'll be a success', because it just doesn't work that way. We simply let things take their natural course. In the beginning we both just let ourselves drift, trying out one thing and another, floating along with the current until we ended up in a stream that suited us. It took some time before we realised which direction we wanted to swim, but from that moment on we both started to work, consciously and concertedly, on promoting my personal career.

Marjorie and I the year we met each other for the first time.

MARJORIE

*M*arjorie and I had actually known each other for a long time. She was in my sister Teresia's class in high school, and we first met each other at a St Nicholas party that was held at our house. That evening we – all Teresia's brothers and sisters – were allowed to help serve lemonade and the traditional almond pastry roll. I had just turned thirteen and was only in the first year of middle school, but I was already head over heals in love with Romy Schneider in the role of Empress Sissi, and therefore not in the least interested in my sister's classmates. Still, there was one among the class of thirty giggling teenagers from the Catholic girls' school, one with dark curly hair and sparkling eyes, who was the only one I noticed.

The curly head in question didn't seem to care about anything that evening but the presents and the traditional poems they'd written about each other. She did remember one thing in particular about that evening, though, as she told me afterwards. Herself an only child, Marjorie – because of course she was the curly head – had gotten the impression that in our large family there were a lot of small fry running around with cake and cookies, all of them little brothers and sisters of her classmate Teresia. And of all those little children she had remembered only one face and only one name: André.

She wasn't much interested in the other sex yet, certainly not in a little squirt like me, and for a long time we lost sight of each other. About six years later I saw Marjorie again, for just a minute, when I dropped Teresia off at her house for a class reunion. Afterwards, whenever I rode past her neighbourhood on my motor scooter on my way to Liège, I used to think to myself, that's where Marjorie lives (not knowing that she'd moved out of her parents' house a long time ago and was now living in student quarters in Nijmegen, where she was studying German at the university). In those days I didn't pay any attention to her, or to any other girls, for that matter. I was much too busy practicing the violin!

Surrounded in Nijmegen by mainly male students, Marjorie seemed to

The first waltz...

have forgotten me, too. Only during the summer holidays in Maastricht did she sometimes bicycle on nice evenings past our house across from the city park, puzzled by vague recollections of someone or other called André. It was not until twelve years after our first meeting that we met again, at a concert given by my sister Teresia, who had meanwhile become a well-known harpist. It was then that the little pilot light still burning in both of us flared up into a great big flame, never to be extinguished.

According to Marjorie I was the embodiment of her romantic ideal of the 'lovable, intelligent – but poor – artist.' (Looking back on things, she must feel deceived as far as that last point is concerned, though some of that is her fault!) On the other hand, she was also the fulfillment of all my dreams: at last I'd found a girl with a sweet disposition and a sense of humour who was also pretty and intelligent. What more could I ask for?

I don't intend to go into our love life any more at this point. Let's just say that we loved each other very much, and that our love has been a source of inspiration for both of us – then, as well as now. Without our love, which has enabled us to collaborate companionably with no trace of competition between us, I would never have made it to the top.

PIZZA PAGANINI

*A*fter I'd been married for a couple of months, I thought it was high time to begin my adolescence. I was about twenty-six at the time. (That is not a typographical error!) Because of my violin studies, I hadn't had time for it at the appropriate age, but apparently everyone has to experience this phase of development at some point.

Ten years too late I donned hippie shirts and started to sport an earring. I also took my violin, which had been my constant companion since the age of five, and stuffed it into the back of a closet. I then locked it, took the key, and threw it in the Maas river. Without even excusing myself to my teacher, André Gertler, I disappeared from the Brussels Conservatory to immerse myself in those things that adolescents are especially good at: hanging around doing nothing, and discussing profound matters like God and the universe. Luckily Marjorie was the breadwinner, otherwise I wouldn't have been able to afford this luxury.

At some point I did realise, though, that I should also contribute something to our upkeep. I don't remember exactly how it came about, maybe it was just because we were both crazy about pizza. At any rate, we suddenly had the idea to open up a pizzeria together. We had a beautiful building in mind, situated in an area of Maastricht full of students and artists, where we were sure to have no lack of customers; besides, at that time there were hardly any pizzerias in the Netherlands.

Considering we had no capital to get us started, we wanted to begin with a stall at the market, where we could take little pizzas we'd made at home and pop them into a mini-oven to warm them up before selling them. Once we'd earned enough money to pay the rent on the building we wanted, we could start our Pizzeria Da André. Marjorie, with her college degree, would be the waitress (she was also suffering from a case of delayed adolescence!), and I – after practicing the violin for more than twenty years – would be the cook. The *pièce de résistance* would be the item on the menu called Pizza Paganini, whereby 'Chef André' himself would come to your table and serenade you personally with a virtuoso piece by Paganini.

49

It was a nice idea, but to be able to play Paganini I had to take my violin out of the closet in double quick time and start practicing again.

So, after an absence of a couple of months, I again put in an appearance at Monsieur Gertler's lessons. His mouth fell open at the sight of me. 'Fantastic! Unbelievable! André, a miracle has happened! Who's been giving you lessons all this time? You've made such incredible progress!'

So you see, adolescence isn't all bad. In fact, it might just
do you a lot of good, even if it hits you a bit late! Let this be some
consolation to parents who get so upset about their ill-humoured
adolescents: leave them alone, they need to act up for a while,
everything's sure to turn out all right in the end.

PART TWO

THE MAASTRICHT SALON ORCHESTRA

I GLISSANDI

*S*ince my marriage to Marjorie I'd been living in Maastricht again, where, in early 1978, I accidentally ran into a former classmate from the conservatory, the cellist Gemma Serpenti. In the course of our conversation she told me that the director of the conservatory had asked her to form a salon orchestra – a six-piece orchestra consisting of two violins, a viola, a cello, a double bass, and a piano – which was supposed to play light music at a party at his home.

Salon orchestras – also called 'palm-court orchestras' –
were springing up like mushrooms in those days. At one point
there were about four hundred of them in the Netherlands!
The most famous was the Resistentie Orkest,
whose name was a take-off on the Residentie Orkest,
the official orchestra of The Hague, so called because the city is
the residence of the Dutch Government. This group
added a bit of spark to a well-known political talk show called
Haagse Kringen (*Hague Circles*). Whenever a cabinet member had had
the floor too long, the orchestra would start to play and completely
drown out the illustrious speaker until he or she – sometimes
angrily but usually good-naturedly – was forced to
relinquish the microphone.

Gemma Serpenti's pick-up orchestra was called *I Glissandi*,[5] because they'd had to make do with one rehearsal before that first concert of theirs. The musicians, the majority of whom were still students,

---

[5] Glissando is a musical term meaning to glide between notes on your instrument or with your voice. If you do this all the time, however, the result is ear-shatteringly awful. *I Glissandi* were, literally, 'the gliders.'

had such fun playing this kind of music that they decided to continue rehearsing together, even after the director's party. There weren't any more concerts in the offing, but they had fun playing together anyway, and once in a while they learned a new piece.

They had eventually acquired a repertoire of eighteen pieces when the first violinist was offered a job in Amsterdam. I had actually run into Gemma on the very day he was moving. Was it a coincidence, or was it fate? Who can say? In any case, Gemma asked me if I felt like taking over for him. I hardly knew what a salon orchestra was, but I said I'd like to come along to a rehearsal and see what it was like. When we played Lehár's *Gold und Silber (Gold and Silver)* a whole new world opened up for me. I was seized by the beat that was later to become virtually the rhythm of my life: the beat of three-four time, the waltz.

What a revelation it was to play a waltz!
I'd never played music like that during all those years of violin study.
I knew waltzes by Strauss, of course, and operetta music by Kálmán and Lehár. My father had conducted them often enough with The Limburg Symphony Orchestra, mostly on the occasion of Carnival and New Year's concerts.[6] I remember that he always spoke of Johann Strauss with deep respect.
'That man was a genius,' he said. 'Johann Strauss could be inspired by the sound of glasses tinkling in a café and was capable of transcribing that sound into a beautiful waltz.' Since studying at the conservatory, however, I had often noticed that his music was not taken very seriously in classical circles. So there had never been any talk of playing waltzes myself. Later as well, when I'd already been a professional musician for some years, this impression was confirmed again and again. It seemed that I'd been right in thinking that Strauss's music was often looked down upon.
My colleagues were frequently very condescending about it.
Whenever a piece by Johann Strauss was on the program, most of them began moaning about it even before the first rehearsal.
A real shame, and something I still find completely incomprehensible.

[6] Carnival (spelled *Carnaval* in Dutch) is Maastricht's version of Mardi Gras, starting on the seventh Sunday before Easter and continuing through Shrove Tuesday, consisting of three days of parades, festivities, and especially drinking, after which Ash Wednesday ushers in the beginning of Lent.

Strauss's music is simply fantastic; every bar betrays his great skill as a composer. Strauss's waltzes aren't at all easy to play either, so musicians can't complain that they aren't challenging enough. Why all the contempt, then?

I accepted the position of first violin in Gemma's salon orchestra with enthusiasm. In the meantime I had also found a job playing in The Limburg Symphony Orchestra, and to top it all off I was going to become a father! As such, I couldn't afford to waste my time on unprofitable hobbies and wanted to change *I Glissandi* and their informal musical get-togethers into something altogether more serious. Our repertoire had to be expanded and, most importantly, if the ensemble wanted to continue to exist in the long run, it would have to find some engagements. The name no longer suited us either, because it had been a long time since 'gliding' had been our motto.

And so I became not only the orchestra's first violinist, I soon had the irresistible urge to be the boss. This was not necessarily seen as a welcome change by the other, long-standing members of the group, but after the usual teething troubles that any professional ensemble experiences in its early stages, everything began to fall into place. The Maastricht Salon Orchestra existed for nearly twenty years, and some of the musicians I played with at the very beginning are still close friends of mine.

BERLIN
IN THE YEAR 1925

*M*arjorie was also enthusiastic about the new kind of music that had entered our household. Up until then she had only heard me practicing études, violin concertos by Bruch and Bartók, and Bach partitas. She loves classical music, and at that time we enjoyed listening to Ravel's *Mother Goose Suite* or Richard Strauss's *Four Last Songs*, sung by Elisabeth Schwarzkopf. But the music I now started to bring home reminded her of her childhood, when it was customary for her family to listen on Sunday afternoons to the opera concert on Radio Brussels, after which they invariably played her father's old 78s. These records, most of which date from the years between 1920 and 1930, were not only old: they also had a quite remarkable history, which would prove to be of great importance to me as well.

Marjorie's father, born in Berlin in 1907, bought a record player when he was a boy of fifteen. A real portable gramophone with a big horn-shaped speaker on top and a crank on its side that you had to wind up to start the music. Because he actually couldn't afford to buy such an expensive thing, he and a friend of his pooled their resources and bought the record player together, which was then stationed at his house for the first two weeks of every month, and at his friend's house for the last two weeks. The records they bought together were kept in the same way: two weeks at one house, two weeks at the other. This way, in spite of their small budget, they were able to build up a nice collection of records.

Being young, they were naturally interested in the light music and dance tunes of their day, played by orchestras such as Jack Hylton and Adalbert Lutter. But that wasn't all. As inhabitants of Berlin, which at that time was considered the cultural capital of the world, they were lucky enough, in the mid-1920s, to witness the most interesting events at close hand. They were present at the premieres of many plays and operas that went on to become world-famous. In 1928 in the Theatre am Schiffbauerdamm, for example, the first performance took place of Bertolt Brecht's *Threepenny Opera*. The melodies that Kurt Weill composed for it unexpectedly grew into hit songs, the most well-known of which was 'The Ballad of Mack the Knife', a genuine hit that practically everyone could sing or whistle. Such music – original performances with singers like Lotte Lenya – was also included in the record collection belonging to my father-in-law and his friend.

The Roaring Twenties didn't last, unfortunately, and the tide turned as it had never turned before. Marjorie's Jewish grandparents fled to the Netherlands in July 1933, a couple of months after Hitler had come to power. Her grandfather, a textile merchant, founded a factory in Maastricht that made hat linings. (The building is still standing, by the way, a few yards from the house we now live in. On Saturday afternoons the Cub Scouts play there, happily unaware of the history of their club house.)

Within three years Marjorie's grandparents had built up a business which ensured them of a reasonable income, and they were able to send for their three sons and daughter-in-law to come over from Berlin. They couldn't take many possessions along, but my father-in-law's baggage included, in addition to a few essentials and ten marks – you weren't allowed to take more out of the country – his unique record collection. This collection had grown in the meantime to no fewer than three hundred records and contained his friend's share as well, who had left all his things behind and fled to South America, asking my father-in-law to take good care of his records.

My father-in-law started a new life in Maastricht. Shortly after immigrating to the Netherlands he attended a ball in Valkenburg where he met my mother-in-law, who was just as much a music lover as he was. For a while they greatly enjoyed listening to the records he'd brought along, most of which were still not available in the Netherlands.

The joy of knowing each other and the fun they had listening to those records together didn't last long, however, because in the years that followed, life turned more and more into a living hell, in which the only thing that mattered was survival.

In 1942 my father-in-law found – with the help of my mother-in-law, who worked for the Resistance – an address where he could go underground. He couldn't keep his beloved record collection, though, which was about all that he still had from his Berlin days. There was room only for essentials. The rest of his possessions, which included his valuable record collection, had to be stored elsewhere. For reasons of security, both he and his records had to change addresses a number of times during the war.

My father-in-law survived the war, together with his mother and one of his brothers. He married in 1945 and began a new life for the second time. At first he had to keep his nose to the grindstone, because most of the family's possessions had been lost in the war. Thank God he still had his beloved records, and after a while he was able to take up his old hobby of listening to music and collecting records.

His already extensive collection was now expanded to include operas and operettas, popular classics, and a lot of music from the post-war years: American and English dance music, French chansons, international hits, and golden oldies. The all-encompassing repertoire ranged from Barnabas von Gézy to Paul Godwin, and from Richard Tauber and Caruso to Maurice Chevalier, Josephine Baker, and Marlene Dietrich – all together hundreds of fantastic records that the family Marjorie grew up in enjoyed listening to for years, so that she too, in her own way, could not imagine a life without music.

Now, so many years later, that same music – that unique collection of old, scratchy 78s, which already had such a long and impressive history – became the basis of my success.

OLD YELLOWING PAPER

*W*hen I joined the salon orchestra *I Glissandi* and started looking around for pieces to add to our repertoire, Marjorie made me listen to some of the records from her father's collection.

In all honesty I have to admit that I didn't know most of the pieces she played for me, having grown up with nothing but classical music. I had really never heard the *Serenade* by Toselli, any more than I had heard of the waltz called *Wiener Praterleben*, better known as *Sport Palace Waltz*, so called because it was played at the opening of the Berlin Sport Palace. But even though I didn't know the music, I took to it right away, and it immediately became apparent that this was the repertoire I was looking for.

After all these years, those heavy albums with their crackling shellac records were brought down from the attic, more than five hundred of them. Marjorie and I now had to look at them all to judge which ones we might be able to use. Luckily my father-in-law had catalogued his records, so we didn't have to listen to all five hundred of them. We read the titles, and because Marjorie knew most of them she could sing me the melodies. If I liked the tune we laid the record aside for future reference. Like this we found, besides the previously mentioned *Serenade* by Toselli and the *Sport Palace Waltz*, such titles as *Susie, Plaisir d'amour, Blaze Away, La petite Tonkinoise, The Veleta*, and *Salut d'amour*, all of which had once been big hits, but had since been forgotten. *Salut d'amour* by Edward Elgar, for instance, was the theme song of Paul Godwin and his dance band, which was heard regularly on Dutch radio in the 1950s.

We now ran up against an obstacle. Although we had gathered together a considerable repertoire of suitable pieces, when I went to the music store to order the sheet music, it appeared that all of it was out of print. None of it was to be found in Maastricht or Amsterdam or The Hague or any place else in the Netherlands. We even went to countless music stores and antiquarian bookshops in Germany and Belgium and rummaged through huge bins of old yellowing sheet music. But nothing came of our week-long treasure hunt. The music was simply no longer available.

Still, we thought there must be some way to get hold of that old, once-popular music that so many people had played only a generation ago. I decided to turn to our local newspaper. They thought it interesting (and newsworthy!) that Maastricht now had a salon orchestra and said they would help us. They published an article about our ensemble, complete with our photograph, which also served as the official birth announcement of The Maastricht Salon Orchestra. In spite of being underweight at birth (its mini-repertoire consisted of only eighteen pieces), this ensemble was destined to lead a long and mostly happy life.

The newspaper launched a special campaign advertising the brand-new Maastricht Salon Orchestra and published a whole series of articles on salon music in general. The emphasis was on our ensemble, of course, but the articles also dealt with salon orchestras that used to exist in the Netherlands, local musical celebrities of earlier times, and pre-war dance orchestras. By way of illustration, they printed faded photographs and beautiful old engravings. Every article was accompanied by an urgent appeal, directed especially at their older readers, to search their attics and cellars for old sheet music in order to help out a couple of poor musicians.

This campaign resulted, only weeks later, in a truck full of salon music. Unbelievable! It was fantastic to see how enthusiastic everyone was. They sent not only music, but also letters, photographs, and old newspaper articles. Our paper printed as many of these as possible, always with a renewed appeal to send music. So many boxes of music were eventually delivered that we didn't have room for them all in our apartment and had to distribute them among the members of the salon orchestra.

How happy Marjorie and I were! I can still see us sitting on the floor together, the whole room littered with dusty, musty sheet music. We spent weeks looking at all of it piece by piece. Marjorie can't read music well, so this time I had to sing the melodies to her. If she recognised the tune, we put it on a pile to play through later. Not all of it was interesting by any means, and after examining the whole truckload, only a few boxes remained with music that we wanted to rehearse.

During rehearsals it became apparent that we couldn't use a lot of it, simply because it wasn't suited to our ensemble, which still consisted of six musicians. The music that people had sent us was often written either for a large orchestra or for piano only. Finally, of the countless boxes of music, only one pile was left over with about a hundred pieces, which we arranged for our orchestra. And, as fate would have it, all of these first pieces of ours eventually became hits.

I'm still grateful to all the people who sent us music way back then, because without their help, and of course that of the newspaper, it would have been very difficult indeed to build up our own repertoire.

Sometimes Marjorie writes down the nonsense I talk and sometimes I say the sensible things she writes. Like this we've worked together successfully for over thirty-five years, and that's how this book has come about.

Schönbrunn Palace with Vienna in the background, the cradle of most of my music. I love being here! It's a special feeling, walking through streets and gazing up at houses where so many famous composers used to live and work.

The house where we wanted to start our Pizzeria da André. What a pity nothing ever came of it!

I spend all my holidays alone with my family. We love to go on nature walks whatever the season.

Favourite holiday spots: Lake Como (above) and Lake Lucerne (below). On all the pictures taken during this vacation, our son Pierre gave the thumbs-up sign to show that he was having a great time.

Neither of us is fond of 'celebrity parties'.
When we have something to celebrate, we
prefer to do it with friends and family.

We both celebrated our fortieth birthdays in
a big way: wistfully, because it meant saying
a definite goodbye to our youth, but also
full of anticipation – anxiously expecting the
onset of our midlife crises!

Above: Marjorie with her parents and her
friend Suse.

Right: My father, my brother Jean-Philippe,
and my son Pierre.

...dressed in a red robe and white surplice...
I'm the choirboy in the middle with the sloppily tied bow.

'The Cart', the first fore-runner of the 'Strauss-mobile' (below). At the steering wheel is my little brother Jean-Philippe; toward the front, tinkering underneath the 'bonnet', is my brother Robert; and my youngest sister Gaby is at the rear, with me keeping a careful eye on her.

Practice, practice, and more practice!

Marjorie and I at the time we renewed our
acquaintance.

The 'flower power' shirt I wore to demonstrate my delayed adolescence. My long hair is the only thing left from that period.

The elegant, three-piece blue-gray suit I wore when 'peddling the Maastricht Salon Orchestra.

The formal portrait we had printed on the front of our first brochure. It's no wonder there were no reactions, what a bunch of grouches! The Maastricht Salon Orchestra with its first members: cellist Gemma Serpenti, violinist Frans Vermeulen, pianist Paul Coenjaarts, double bass player Pascal Vliegen and myself.

After the Maastricht Salon Orchestra played a Sunday afternoon concert, there was usually time for the five of us to wander around the city.

For years we played at the marvellous Ghent Festival. You can't bring yourself to leave such a beautiful city as soon as the concert is over. With me, from left to right: Irene Houben, Tjeu Heyltjes, a representative of the 'Ministry of Festivities' (too bad this post doesn't exist in the Netherlands!), Frans Vermeulen, and Klaartje Polman.

Tired and acting a bit silly after the Hieringebiete Concert in Maastricht (from left to right: Jean, Frans, myself, Gemma and Paul).

Also in Ghent, here with Marjorie.

WILL YOU SAY SOMETHING?
I DON'T DARE!

*B*esides seeing to the artistic development of The Maastricht Salon Orchestra, it was of the utmost importance to take the organisational side of things firmly in hand. Looking for music, arranging it, and rehearsing it was a lot of fun, but eventually we wanted to play all that beautiful music for an audience.

I temporarily traded in my modern 'flower power' clothes – which I still wore at the time, though they didn't exactly fit in with my new 'salon' image – for a respectable, blue-grey, three-piece suit, and went in search of customers.

Considering we played music of 'the good old days,' I started out by visiting the directors of various nursing homes. The elderly would especially enjoy listening to our music, I thought. Most of the directors were in fact happy to accept my proposal and said they would be glad to let us play a concert at their institutions. They couldn't afford to pay us much, but that wasn't the point. The most important thing, in my opinion, was being able to perform.

One of the directors was so enthusiastic that he invited us to play a concert on the first Sunday of every month for a whole year. This was an enormous challenge. We worked like crazy rehearsing all those new pieces that people had sent us in response to the newspaper campaign, so that we could offer them a new program every month.

It became obvious to us that there were certain pieces, such as that wonderful *Serenade* by Toselli, that people could never get enough of. From the very beginning this piece was part of every program, and would later prove to be immensely important for the career of The Maastricht Salon Orchestra.

One thing led to another and suddenly things started to take off. At every concert we gave, someone was present in the audience who invited us to play another concert. Soon nursing homes and rehabilitation centres would have to make way for concert halls and theatres. But I'll never forget that it was there, in the presence of all those elderly people, most of whom probably aren't even alive anymore, that the career of

The Maastricht Salon Orchestra was born. It was there that I realised for the first time how much music can mean to people. You can make people really happy with music, driving away their sorrow, pain, and loneliness for a while and giving them the illusion, at least for a couple of hours, of a better life.

This, incidentally, is a goal I still strive toward in my concerts:
to let people forget their cares and enjoy themselves for a whole
evening, so that they go home thinking that life isn't so bad after all.
Luckily, from the many enthusiastic reactions I receive,
I get the idea that I generally succeed in doing this.

About this time I also began talking a bit between the pieces. I felt that the audience wanted something more than just music. They wanted to know who those people playing the instruments were, for example. I also felt funny just walking out there in silence and starting to play the first piece with no preliminary pleasantries to smooth the way. When you make an entrance somewhere, aren't you supposed to greet everyone first? In the beginning, though, I was so shy I could hardly get a word out. The first time I even asked Gemma, the cellist, if she would please say something to the audience. But Gemma would rather play than talk, so there was nothing else to do but say something myself. Before long I noticed that people reacted enthusiastically when I talked a bit before playing, and that my small talk made them listen more attentively to the music, simply because contact had been established between the musicians and the audience.

During those first concerts in nursing homes I talked about ordinary, everyday things, such as our family life, and especially about our first baby that was on its way. When Marc was finally born we had to take him along to every concert to be oohed and aahed at by all the nursing-home residents.

The better I got at telling stories, the more I dared to digress from the domestic sphere, and I began to relate interesting facts about the music itself. At first these talks were improvised – things I thought up during the concert itself – but gradually we started preparing the text of my remarks together at home. Sometimes Marjorie wrote something down that we then worked on together, making changes here and there to fit my 'style'; sometimes we wrote a text together from scratch. This is actually how we still do things today.

This talking between the pieces became more and more important to me, until it eventually became an essential part of my concerts. Once, by way of experiment – because of course you keep experimenting and polishing up your act, so that it doesn't get stale – I tried to give a concert in silence, abandoning for one evening the 'talky' style I'd developed. The shivers run down my spine when I think back on it now! There was such a horrible tenseness in the hall, such an icy atmosphere that I'll never do it again! This contact with the audience, established with that small talk of mine between numbers, is something I can no longer do without.

The Maastricht Salon Orchestra serenading my grandmother on her 100th birthday!

THE FIRST FULL HOUSE

*A*t first the agenda of The Maastricht Salon Orchestra was completely filled with concerts in nursing homes, as well as rehearsals to expand our repertoire. Because we still didn't have enough money to rent a studio, we rehearsed at Gemma's parents' house, in a room in the attic. Marjorie always came along, mostly because she thought it was fun – sometimes she sat there knitting baby clothes for Marc – but also to listen with a critical ear, occasionally making a comment or offering a helpful suggestion. She was, after all, the only one who already knew our 'new' repertoire; the other members of the salon orchestra had all grown up with classical music as I had and were therefore not well acquainted with this type of light music.

After a while we could finally play so many new pieces that I was ready to venture further afield and attempt a concert outside our usual circuit of nursing homes. A photographer made a formal portrait of our ensemble, in which we sat, dressed in clothes of the period, surrounded by old-fashioned furniture and knick-knacks (borrowed from our grandparents) that gave the impression of a genuine old salon. We had a couple of hundred brochures printed with this elegant photograph of the five of us – the viola player had meanwhile left the salon orchestra – printed on the front. Marjorie wrote the accompanying text, recommending us as the ideal group to provide light music at weddings and parties. We then sent the brochure to more than three hundred establishments in the area, including some in Belgium, which is just around the corner from Maastricht, so to speak.

Because salon music was making a comeback at the time, we were hoping for a lot of positive reactions. We sat at home, eagerly awaiting replies, for weeks and weeks. There weren't any, though. Not even one. We might just as well have dumped all those brochures in the Maas. (A lot of things I thought I didn't need anymore had already been swallowed up by that river!) Apparently this wasn't the right way to bring

69

our salon orchestra to the people. So I took my three-piece suit out of the closet again and went off to visit some theatre managers. This was no easy task. It proved to be almost impossible to get an appointment to see any of them, let alone to persuade one of them to give us an engagement. Such people won't condescend to talk to an artist whose name they don't know.

Fortunately, I was finally able to get through to a couple of people. Matthew Schmeitz, then director of the Wijngracht Theatre and the Roda Hall in Kerkrade, rather liked the idea and engaged us for a Christmas concert at the magnificent, romantic Erenstein Castle in Kerkrade. Like a loving father, he was present in person on the appointed day to receive us and to welcome the audience as his guests. I can still see him looking around before the concert to make sure everything was all right, straightening a tablecloth here, tidying up a Christmas decoration there, and lighting candles on all the tables. Musicians find such behaviour heartwarming. I still hate having to play in a theatre where there's absolutely no one to welcome you. It's like being invited to someone's home for coffee: there's the coffee on the table, even a slice of triple-layer cake next to it, but the hostess herself has gone shopping. There's nothing more unpleasant than such a display of bad manners!

That first concert in Kerkrade on Christmas Day was such a huge success that afterwards Matthew Schmeitz invited us to give one or more concerts every year, even after he had taken a new job as director of the Maaspoort Theatre in Venlo. Even now, after all my success both in the Netherlands and internationally, he watches over the quality of my performances like a sort of godfather, occasionally coming to see me in the office 'to go over things,' as he says.

Another theatre that finally agreed to give us an engagement after several unsuccessful sales pitches on my part was the Bonbonnière in Maastricht. At first the director was rather skeptical about the whole venture, but he wanted to help me all the same, and came up with what he thought was a good idea.

In Maastricht's beautiful old theatre there was at that time a series of lunch concerts on Wednesday afternoons, where people could enjoy listening to chamber music between 12 and 2 p.m. while eating the sandwiches they'd brought along and drinking a cup of coffee. The series had been well attended for years, except on Ash Wednesday, the day after the official end of Carnival, when of course no one in Maastricht – that bastion of Carnival celebrants – was in the mood to listen to chamber music. On this day every right-minded Carnavalist (and in Maastricht this means the majority of the population) is lying in bed with a terrible hangover, and classical music is probably the last thing in the world he or she wants to listen to. Perhaps this day would be especially suitable for a concert by The Maastricht Salon Orchestra. Instead of a cup of coffee and their own sandwiches, the public would drink beer and eat pickled herring, the world's best remedy for a hangover!

This idea gave the concert its title: Hieringebiete Concert. By way of explanation for the uninitiated, *hieringe* is Maastricht dialect for 'herring' and *biete* means 'bite.' This is what one generally does in Maastricht on Ash Wednesday, when you can get herring in every café as an antidote for your hangover. This has the immediate effect of inducing you to order another beer, to wash down the sour taste of the herring, and, as this cycle repeats itself, Ash Wednesday in Maastricht gets more enjoyable as the day goes on! I don't go in much for celebrating Carnival myself, but I must say that the atmosphere in Maastricht on Ash Wednesday is certainly unique.

The idea of a Hieringebiete Concert appealed to me. In any case I thought it worthwhile to give it a try. In the meantime we'd had posters made from the same photograph that we'd had printed on our brochure, and all the members of The Maastricht Salon Orchestra hurried into town to hang up posters everywhere. Once again we anxiously awaited the result. Would this have more effect than the three hundred brochures we'd sent out? Or would we again wait in vain?

This time the response was overwhelming! On Ash Wednesday 1979, the day we gave our first Hieringebiete Concert, the Redoute (the café area of the theatre which was used for lunch concerts) was full to overflowing. As was customary at these concerts, about 150 chairs had been set up. These were all occupied, while all around them more than 400 people were packed in, and some even had to listen from outside.

The concert was a huge success! The audience enjoyed every note we played. They had a wonderful time, applauded wildly, and completely forgot about their hangovers.

This, then, appeared to be the ideal solution to the Ash Wednesday lunch concert, and afterwards the Maastricht theatre renewed our engagement every year.

Including that first time The Maastricht Salon Orchestra gave eighteen Hieringebiete Concerts. The audience that was then 500 strong grew to more than 5000, and the concert was no longer attended only by 'Maastrichtenaren.' People came from far and wide for this unique experience.

The quaint Redoute hall quickly became too small for the 'herring biters' – the people were packed in like sardines! After trying out ever-larger halls, we finally arrived at the enormous hall of Maastricht's convention centre, the MECC. For many years we gave our

Hieringebiete Concert every Ash Wednesday for thousands of appreciative fans, and pickled herring was always very much a part of our offering!

Now, thirty years later, we sometimes look back and remember how we used to say to each other: if only we could give a concert like this on the Vrijthof, in summer, outside... that would be so wonderful!

PICKLED HERRING
AND CAMEMBERT,
GINGERBREAD AND HORSE-DUNG

*T*he Ash Wednesday Hieringebiete Concert, the yearly Christmas concert, and the occasional performance of The Maastricht Salon Orchestra could not provide the financial basis to support five families, so I kept on trying to put together a plan to sell more concerts. In the early years of our ensemble, though, theatre managers weren't so sure what to think of me. I badgered them constantly, trying to persuade them that The Maastricht Salon Orchestra was so special that they just had to include us in their season program. Most of the theatre managers were dismissive; only one or two saw something in it and reluctantly agreed to give us a concert. But in what category would it fall? In what kind of series did a salon orchestra like mine belong? The general opinion seemed to be that we really only played background music suitable for dinners and parties! That was the one thing we didn't want to do, though; I was convinced that my salon orchestra was ready for the stage.

Now that I'm more at home in the business, I realise how difficult it was for those theatre managers to give us engagements. They get so many requests for concerts from all variety of artists. Every day they're swamped with offers from rising stars, while at the same time they're under pressure to include existing celebrities in their program. Especially as far as music is concerned, they're often tied to an existing series, like coffee concerts on Sunday mornings, chamber music evenings, concerts of operetta music, or recitals that are given on fixed evenings. A group like The Maastricht Salon Orchestra didn't really fit into any of these categories, and in those days it would have been presumptuous to call it a 'special concert.'

Apparently I was so persistent in nagging them that a few of the more inventive theatre managers instigated a new 'tradition,' both to do me a favour and to get me off their back. At that time they didn't yet know what I thought I knew – that they were doing the theatre-goers even more of a favour than they were doing me!

If I didn't want to play background music at dinner parties, though, then the organisers thought that at least there should be something to eat at my concerts, otherwise this kind of music would be unpalatable! And so they thought up all kinds of delicacies with which to serve up The Maastricht Salon Orchestra in the most appetizing way possible. The fare varied from pickled herring and Christmas cookies to hot chocolate, asparagus, and French cheese – fortunately not necessarily in those combinations. (By the way, we actually ended up playing at quite a few dinner parties. After all, we had to eat, too!)

If you ask me, all those delicious offerings weren't at all necessary, the public would have enjoyed our concerts tremendously without the trimmings. From the very beginning, practically all of the concert halls were sold out, and that couldn't have been due to the refreshments. It was just that there was some sort of framework necessary in which to place The Maastricht Salon Orchestra and the combination of Maastricht and culinary delights (pickled herring?) is almost always a big success.

In this way several wonderful traditions came into being, some of which continued to exist for many years. For example, for years we

Our poses might look a bit forced in this picture, but the fun we were having was real! From left to right: Henriette Janssen, Jean Sassen, Frans Vermeulen, myself, and Jo Huijts.

played a New Year's Concert – to the delight of a great many people – in a packed theatre in Heerlen, a town about fifteen miles from Maastricht. The atmosphere at this concert was really something special. A slight hangover from New Year's Eve, combined with the fact that most of them had only had half a night's sleep, meant that the audience was always in an unusual mood, prone to both hysterical laughter and tearful weeping. The tears fell copiously during each melancholy melody, and my jokes were greeted with more laughter than on other days. In the intermission, instead of getting a cup of coffee and a cookie, the audience was given a glass of champagne. The people who had made their New Year's resolutions just a few hours before now had time to forget them and could doze off blissfully with their heads full of melancholy music.

Another 'yummy' concert that we gave for ten years was the Mother's Day Concert, also in the theatre in Heerlen – for a long time the only large theatre in the south of the Netherlands – at which all the mothers in the audience were presented with cakes and chocolates. You can imagine what a hit this was with the mothers, who had just had to endure breakfast in bed, with burned toast and runny or rock-hard eggs so lovingly prepared by their spouse and children.

The most delightful of all these tasty musical events were the 'Speculaas' Concert. After a cautious beginning about thirty years ago in a provincial theatre in central Limburg, we eventually gave about ten of these concerts in the weeks leading up to the feast of St Nicholas on 6 December.[7]

The unique tradition of holding the 'Speculaas' Concert on the Sunday before 6 December began in those days with a cookie and a cup of coffee, served by two Black Peters, St Nick's Moorish servants. Just like the Hieringebiete Concert, this fun family concert developed into a huge affair, growing into a veritable St Nicholas show.

The first Black Peters were played by the girls from the box office. As far as I can remember, St Nicholas himself didn't even make an appearance at that first concert. We played our salon music and the audience loved it. (They also enjoyed eating cookies during the intermission; I don't want to detract from that part of the concert!) After that first time, something special was added to the concert every year, a funny act

---

[7] This is an important holiday in the Netherlands. St Nicholas and his helpers, called Black Peters because they are Moors, bring children and grown-ups alike candy and also presents. Speculaas, traditionally eaten at this time, are spiced cookies resembling a thinner, crunchier version of gingerbread.

starring St Nicholas and his helpers. Each time we all helped to think up something new, trying not to forget that the music was the most important part, because that's what the people had come for, to hear the music.

It's really fantastic to be able to do something like this, both the preparations – which we enjoyed enormously, of course – and the concerts themselves. Seeing everyone in the audience, children and grown-ups alike, enjoying themselves and roaring with laughter, is a wonderful experience that we all enjoyed year after year.

All kinds of 'St Nicks' performed with us. At first they only appeared as dignified, saintly men with deep voices who welcomed the children and announced that there would be cookies to eat in the intermission. Later on, though, we invited some artist or other to play the role, and quite a few extremely talented saints appeared with us: the Dutch roller-skating champion – wearing a bishop's mitre and red robe with gold trim – accompanied by a whole club of roller-skating Black Peters, offered an impressive display of acrobatics. The comedian Pierre Cnoops, in the guise of St Nicholas, galloped across the stage on horseback, but the minute he opened his mouth everyone recognised his voice and funny way of talking, and peals of laughter filled the hall. The tenor Andrea Poddighe sang a beautiful Italian duet in a Venetian gondola with a darling little 'soprano Peter.' Wim Steinbusch, a talented actor as well as singer, performed the part for several years running, as an Austrian, a Mexican, and even a somewhat arrogant English St Nicholas, who actually played a tennis match against a groaning 'Peter Seles'!

In later years, more and more children started coming to these concerts, and the program was especially geared to them. A terribly naughty but very talented Black Peter in the person of the versatile clarinettist Manoe Konings regularly stole the show.

In order to accomplish these things on stage you need a vast crew of technicians to build the set and to provide special effects, such as having a gondola glide across the stage. You need lighting and sound technicians, a truck and driver to transport all the equipment, a wardrobe mistress, and a make-up artist.

For many years, though, we didn't have enough money for any of these things. We could get by on my salary from The Limburg Symphony Orchestra and the money I earned playing with The Maastricht Salon Orchestra, but we couldn't afford to invest in trucks, stage sets, rehearsal halls, costumes, and technical personnel. So we did as much as possible ourselves, Marjorie and I and the members of The Maastricht Salon Orchestra.

Sometimes I swore at myself, like the time I had the stupid idea to have the Austrian St Nicholas and seven Black Peters come on stage on cross-country skis during the Skaters' Waltz. And I wasn't the only one swearing – everyone who almost broke their legs stumbling around on those awful things was swearing too! Once I get an idea in my head, though, no one can talk me out of it. Skiing was on the program, and skiing it had to be, and on cross-country skis to boot. My just reward was having to drag eight pairs of skis around during that whole tour, unloading them from the car and lugging them inside, then hauling them out again for the trip to the next theatre. If you want to start your own business, you have to tackle any problem that presents itself, you can't afford to be choosy.

Luckily Marjorie is of the same opinion, as witnessed by her taking matters firmly in hand that time St Nick's horse had to wait in the wings too long and ended up leaving his mark behind. I had even turned around a couple of times while playing to see where the stench was coming from. The people in the front rows had also begun to fidget, eyeing each other suspiciously: who was the one who had eaten too much onion soup before the concert? Marjorie detected the cause of the unrest, noticed that no one else intended to do anything about it, and happily set about sweeping up the steaming horse-dung herself. This would have left a true horse-lover 'cold', perhaps, but, believe me, Marjorie found it a memorable experience!

THE NIGHTINGALE

*L*adies and gentleman, once upon a time there was an Italian musician who fell in love. Yes, well, this often happens to musicians.

He fell in love with a German princess.

It's true... What I'm telling you is really true ... Everything I say is true, of course. But this is really, really true!

This German princess was terribly rich, and the musician was ... like all musicians... as poor as a church mouse. The princess was so rich, and he was so poor, that she didn't want to have anything to do with him. But he was so much in love with her that he wanted to give her a present. And so he wrote a piece of music for her. This piece of music became world-famous. And nothing was heard of the princess ever again.

Ladies and gentlemen, we're going to play for you... composed by an Italian musician ... for a German princess... and performed by five ... poor ... musicians: the *Serenade* by Toselli!

With this true 'mini fairytale' I have often announced the truly world-famous *Serenade* by Toselli. As I mentioned earlier, this beautiful, melancholy melody – which I've been playing for many years with the greatest pleasure – was of decisive importance for The Maastricht Salon Orchestra.

When I was searching for repertoire for our ensemble in the truckload of yellowing sheet music that we'd received thanks to those advertisements in the newspaper, one of the pieces I found was the *Serenade* opus 6 by Enrico Toselli. The name didn't mean a thing to me. Lots of people might be surprised at this, but the fact remains that I'd grown up only with classical music. Marjorie said she knew the piece well, however, so I played it through to hear what it was like. I was crazy about it right from the start. We rehearsed it with the salon orchestra, and I put it on the program for the next concert in the nursing home.

And what a success it turned out to be! How enthusiastic the people were! I can still picture it, all those happy old

The record sleeve we designed for *Rendez-vous*. The Maastricht Salon Orchestra as it existed for the first five years: Frans Vermeulen, second violin; Jean Sassen, double bass; Paul Coenjaarts, piano; Gemma Serpenti, cello; and myself. People always look so serious in old photographs, which was our reason for doing so here. In reality things were much more fun than this picture suggests!

people, softly humming along with that melody they knew so well. After that the *Serenade* by Toselli was never missing from a concert. Even when it wasn't officially on the program, we played it as an encore, not only in those first concerts in nursing homes, but also later on, when we'd been playing for years to packed theatres.

When we made our first record, it went without saying that the *Serenade* by Toselli would be on it. Although this piece had been played and recorded many times before – by orchestras such as that led by Barnabas von Gézy – it had sunk into obscurity like so many other 'hits' from that time.

Because we couldn't get a big record company to take us on – who's interested in an unknown ensemble that plays old salon music? – we recorded our first record on our own.

'On our own' actually meant 'with our own money,' at least as much as we could cough up. In those days we really were poor musicians. We found a studio that was willing to make a record with us for 14,000 guilders, which at that time was just over £4,000. It seemed like a fortune. How on earth could we manage to conjure up that amount?

Each member of the salon orchestra therefore went about drawing up a list with the names of family members, friends, and acquaintances who would be willing to buy the record when it was finally released. We thought we could come up with about fifty customers each, and we also planned to sell the record at our concerts. We borrowed a bit of money here and there, and after a while we were ready to take the plunge. A thousand records were made at the first pressing.

To our great surprise the records sold like hot cakes; people bought them at concerts, sometimes five at a time. It was unbelievable! In no time at all we'd sold every last one, thereby recovering the costs of our first big investment and enabling us to pay off our debts. That first record of ours – which was named *Rendez-vous* after The Maastricht Salon Orchestra's theme song – was eventually reissued fifteen times.

Naturally it was important to be able to sell those records: we needed the money to live on, although that wasn't my only objective. I saw the record more as a highly suitable means of circulating our music and making it known to a wider public.

On my own, I started up a promotion campaign directed at all the radio stations in the area. The music producers often looked at me in astonishment. For years they'd been broadcasting the classical concerts given by The Limburg Symphony Orchestra conducted by my father, and now suddenly the son of this well-known conductor was asking them to play a record with salon music. In their eyes it was scandalous, to say the least, and many others thought the same.

The first television performances with The Maastricht Salon Orchestra in the early 1980s. New Year's Eve show broadcast by Belgian Radio and Television from the Astoria Hotel in Brussels. Talks and interviews were broadcast alternately with our music (in the photo are Ministers Martens and De Clerq). Millions of people watched this program and it contributed a great deal to our popularity in Belgium.

First performance on Dutch television for the program *Van Gewest tot Gewest* (*From Region to Region*), presented with great enthusiasm by the late Huub Mans, who loved our music so much that he would have liked best to play along with us!

I didn't listen to their objections and simply left a record with them, firmly convinced that, sooner or later, they'd end up playing it. Sometimes you have premonitions about such things.

Luckily not everyone reacted so negatively. I met with a lot of enthusiasm at the BRT (Belgian Radio and Television) in Hasselt, just over the border in Belgian Limburg. The chief producer, Paul Cabus, thought I might be on to something, in spite of the fact that he had also broadcast a lot of my father's concerts. He even organised a live radio concert with The Maastricht Salon Orchestra.

The reaction was tremendous! Dozens of people phoned the studio before the concert had even finished to ask which orchestra was playing, and if it had made any records. For us, of course, it was a great reward for our efforts and an incentive to continue in this vein; for the radio it was a reason to play our record more frequently from then on.

The Belgian Radio and Television remained faithful to us. In the years that followed they continued to play our first record regularly, as well as those we made later. And so it happened – oh happy day! – that the music producer, Irene Houben, was looking for music for a program presented by the well-known Belgian radio announcer Jos Ghysen and listened to 'our' *Serenade* by Toselli.

While Irene, sunk in reverie, was listening to this romantic music, the bird in the cage on her desk began to chirp along. Only after the last chord had died away did the bird stop singing. Irene woke with a start from her daydream. She looked in amazement at the bird in the cage, then turned questioningly to Jos. They asked themselves if it had been a coincidence.

They decided to put it to the test and played the *Serenade* by Tosellionce more. Again the bird began to sing. Apparently this was such beautiful music that even a bird enjoyed it so much that it started to sing along. It was a unique combination, the mingling of those lovely sounds, and Irene hurried off to the radio station's archives in search of a tape of birdsong.

She found what she was looking for, a tape with the beautiful song of the nightingale, taped by a Belgian soldier during a lonely night watch. In the studio they made a mix of the nightingale and our recording of Toselli and, lo and behold, a hit was born!

Jos broadcast the 'new' serenade on his program, and although it was meant partly as a joke, the telephone didn't stop ringing. What was that beautiful piece of music, the listeners wanted to know. Was it a record? Where could you get it? The people at the radio had intuitively come up with the ideal combination of a super-romantic melody and the fairytale-like song of the nightingale.

Jos told us about the enthusiastic reactions of the listeners, where-upon I decided to look for a record producer who wanted to record this beautiful piece. In the Netherlands I drew a blank – the Dutch just aren't a romantic people – but at PolyGram in Brussels I met the pro-ducer Paul Moens. Sighing a great deal – and muttering things like the 'Serenade by Toselli? But, my dear fellow, I've got dozens of recordings of it, whole cupboards full' – Paul nevertheless let himself be talked into recording it. At last I'd found a 'real' record company, even if it was only going to make a single.

At first The Maastricht Salon Orchestra, including Marjorie and me, had its doubts about the whole project. We all thought it sounded fine, the serenade with that birdsong and all, but could we as classical musicians afford to make a record of it? Well, we all thought it was a bit of a joke, actually. The double bass player, Jean, was the only one who

Our first Gold Record – *Serenata* – presented during the *'HIERINGEBIETE' CONCERT* by the mayor of Maastricht, Mr Baeten. Just behind him to the left and right are the commentator Huub Mans and the actor Pieke Dassen.

thought it was really good. He was convinced it would be a success, and he turned out to be right.

Jos Ghysen played the single – which was, after all, a product of his program – nearly every week on the radio, making the 'Serenade with the Nightingale' known and loved in all of Belgium. After only a few weeks it climbed to the Top Ten, and there our bird continued to chirp for months. The single became an LP, *Serenata*, and in no time it also won a place in the hit parade. Before long we received our first Gold Record, the crowning glory of our first five years of effort.

LAUGHTER
AND
TEARS

*S*ometimes people don't realise that an artist's heyday is preceded by years of hard work. Life is certainly not easy for a musician on the rocky road to fame. Between the occasional peaks are deep valleys that have to be crossed as well. Luckily, the long path leading to my current, overwhelming success has generally been a steady, uphill climb. This is not to say, however, that besides the many successful and enjoyable concerts there were not some less successful performances.

Two concerts in Germany will always stick in my mind, one of them because it was one of the most amusing performances we ever gave, in spite of a small accident, and the other because it was the biggest disaster ever experienced by The Maastricht Salon Orchestra.

During the heyday of The Maastricht Salon Orchestra – the years immediately following the success of the '*Serenade* with the Nightingale' – we regularly gave concerts in Germany. In those days the members of the orchestra were Frans Vermeulen, second violin, Jean Sassen, double bass, Tjeu Heyltjes, piano, and various women who took turns playing the cello. To clarify the situation, perhaps I should say that I was still the first violin.

Those concert trips to Germany, which usually took place on Sundays,[8] were unique. Our wives often came along too, so that these trips, far from being only serious work, also had the air of a pleasure trip being taken by a large family. After the concert we usually took a walk through the city in question, after which we had a nice meal somewhere before starting the journey home. Like this we often spent all the money we'd just earned playing the concert, but that didn't bother us. We'd played well and we'd made a lot of people happy with our music, that was the important part. Besides, we had lots of fun together on these trips.

---

[8] Sunday was generally a free day for the members of The Limburg Symphony Orchestra, in which Jean (principal double bass), Frans, and I played.

At a concert in Trier one Sunday the *Sport Palace Waltz* was one of the pieces on the program. When I announce this waltz I always invite the audience to participate. I don't tell them exactly what it is that's expected of them, only that they should pay close attention to Frans, the second violinist. During the refrain of this waltz you're supposed to whistle on your fingers, and Frans can do this better than anyone. When I announce this piece Frans always stands up and points to himself, so the audience knows who I'm talking about. On that Sunday in Trier, at the moment I started to say, 'Just watch Frans, then you'll know exactly what to do,' a floor plank came loose and Frans fell with a loud crash through the stage, chair and all. The audience, assuming that this was supposed to happen, burst out laughing. Frans lay on the floor, half-sunk through the hole in the stage, and the only thing you could see from the hall were his legs thrashing around. Luckily he hadn't hurt himself, but there was great consternation on all sides. Stage hands rushed in immediately to repair the damage, but this took quite some time. We all stayed where we were and I chatted a bit with the audience to bridge the unexpected gap in the program.

When everything was fixed, we wanted to continue playing where we'd left off, so I said again, 'Just watch Frans, then you'll know exactly what to do,' whereupon the audience again burst into such uncontrollable laughter that it was impossible for us to go on. I let them laugh till they'd had enough and waited until it was completely silent again.

Just when, in all seriousness, I finally raised my bow to start playing again, I suddenly started laughing. In fact, I had such hysterics I could not stop, I laughed till the tears were running down my face. Frans and the other members of the orchestra couldn't hold back any longer either and there they sat, roaring with laughter, until they'd infected the audience with it again and the whole hall was cracking up for the third time. It took a long time for things to quiet down enough for us to go on playing.

Such things aren't supposed to happen, of course, but it was immense fun, and for many years we were asked back to play in Trier. I learned my lesson, though: I never give a concert anymore without inspecting the stage beforehand!

After a concert in Amsterdam. From left to right: Frans Vermeulen, Gemma Serpenti, myself, Jean Sassen, and Tjeu Heyltjes.

Around the mid-1980s political policy in both the Netherlands and Germany was strongly directed at bringing the arts 'to the people', in other words, making 'culture' accessible to a much broader public. This was of course an admirable idea, and one I was only too glad to promote, but unfortunately the methods used to reach this goal were sometimes ill-chosen, to say the least.

For example, I still remember the time The Limburg Symphony Orchestra made a tour of the former mining villages of the province of Limburg, giving concerts on street corners and public squares – the whole orchestra dressed in long black dresses and tails and seated on a giant semi-trailer. In this way they hoped to reach 'the people' – those who would normally never go near a concert hall – and introduce them to classical music. I don't know how successful they were. The musicians, in any case, were not at all happy about this 'semi series', for which only a handful of people showed up in each village.

As part of this same scheme to bring culture to the people, The Maastricht Salon Orchestra was once engaged by the Dutch embassy in Bonn to play a concert somewhere in Germany. In those days we often worked closely with the embassy, and the concerts they had organised for us so far had always been very successful.

This concert in Germany was also the last one that our pianist Tjeu Heyltjes was to play with us. To our great sorrow he had decided to leave The Maastricht Salon Orchestra, after having played with us for more than five years. This was to be his farewell concert, and he was also finding it difficult. We had spent some wonderful years together, and his irrepressible sense of humour had always contributed to the fantastic atmosphere in the orchestra.

On the way to Germany that day, therefore, we were already in a rather melancholy mood. The irony of fate would see to it that this would be one of the most joyless concerts, in all respects, that we ever gave. I don't remember the name of the place the embassy had sent us to, but it was an ugly, remote industrial town somewhere in the Ruhr region.

The town had seen better days, that much was immediately apparent when we drove into it on that drizzly, overcast Sunday morning. It looked drab, dilapidated, and abandoned. An aura of gloom hung over it, there was not a person to be seen, and we asked ourselves why on earth the embassy had sent us to such a place.

Our mood didn't improve at the sight of such sombreness. Perhaps we'd made a mistake. Maybe there was another place with the same name and we'd accidentally ended up in the wrong town. In that case the embassy should have warned us. It was obvious that something was wrong.

Thanks to my colleagues' sense of humour I did see the comedy of the situation, but in the meantime I was also becoming very nervous. I'm always well-prepared for my concerts, and I want each one of them to be a success. But how would I fare here? And where on earth was the theatre or concert hall? We couldn't even find some kind of community centre in this desolate ghost town, and the few people we came across knew nothing about a concert. What a joke!

At last we arrived at a square where a tent had been set up. A few Turkish children were wandering around, obviously with nothing better to do than be bored. Someone told us that a 'Sunday concert' was supposed to take place in the tent, so we thought that had to be us.

Cautiously, we went inside to have a look around. The tent itself was quite nice, a so-called 'mirror tent', small but pleasant enough, and there was actually a piano standing in the corner. In the middle was a wooden dance floor (help!) and all around, next to the walls, were booths where the audience could sit, that is, if anyone showed up. Five minutes before the concert was due to start there wasn't a soul in sight. My nightmare had come true! During all my years with The Maastricht

Salon Orchestra nothing, but nothing, had seemed worse to me than having to perform to an empty hall. It had always been my greatest fear. Completely unfounded, of course, because until then we'd only played for well-filled halls. Now, however, in this Godforsaken hole, the unthinkable was about to happen.

I broke out in a cold sweat. We stood there, plucking nervously on our instruments, when – thank heavens! – two elderly couples sauntered in and sat down. Because it was already ten minutes after the concert was supposed to have started, we decided to go ahead and play something, for those four people, ourselves, and our wives who had come along.

When you think about it, it was really funny. You drive almost two hundred miles, having rehearsed beforehand to play a concert for maybe several hundred people, you change your clothes, and then there you are, all five of you in tails or evening gown, feeling like a laughing stock.

While we were playing, the Turkish children and someone who in the old days would have been known as the 'village idiot' came and stood in the entrance. I looked meaningfully at them, trying to encourage them to come closer, and when the piece was finished, I asked them if they'd enjoyed it. The man muttered something to himself, and from the children's reaction I figured out that they didn't understand any German.

They seemed to like being there in the tent anyway, because they decided to stay, and after a while they began to feel so much at home that they started to play a game of tag on the dance floor. This made an enormous racket, but we played on through thick and thin. I tried to make it clear to them that if they would only sit still and listen, they would enjoy the concert much more. After all, they were our audience that morning and we felt responsible for them. They didn't understand our good intentions, though, and continued to stomp around happily on the wooden planks.

At last we gave up, apologised to the two couples, and fled from the fiasco, which had been enough to strike terror into the heart of any self-respecting musician. It was only when we were on the highway again, driving home, that we could take a deep breath and laugh about the whole thing. What a disaster that had been! We'd never experienced anything like it, and we fervently hoped that nothing like it would ever happen again.

The bright side of the story was that because of this debacle our good friend Tjeu was honestly able to say a heartfelt farewell that day. 'André, old boy' he said, 'take my advice and break with the embassy!'

We didn't have to go to such extremes, but by now it should be obvious that the cultural policy described above certainly had its drawbacks.

SAVE THE SAHEL REGION

*T*he fate of the world's poor and environmental protection are two problems that Marjorie and I both take very much to heart, and for this reason I would like to devote a chapter of this book to a very special concert.

Shortly after the Hieringebiete Concert of 1987, Sjef Vink, a commentator for Radio Limburg, phoned me to ask if I would be willing to discuss a benefit concert. Sjef is a member of the Maastricht-Niou Committee,[9] which concerns itself with the welfare of the people in the African country of Burkina Faso, one of the poorest countries in the Sahel region along the southern range of the Sahara. He was so enthusiastic about the Hieringebiete Concert that an idea had taken root in his mind to raise funds for this committee and the good cause it supported by means of such a concert. Hundreds of people attended the concerts of The Maastricht Salon Orchestra, so he thought it would be a good way to raise money for Niou. The idea appealed to me immediately, especially because I also saw it as a means of contributing to the improvement of the environment.

I wanted to give a concert with the motto 'Save the Sahel region – plant a tree for ten guilders!', the proceeds of which would all go to Burkina Faso for the purpose of planting trees. In this way we hoped to make part of the increasingly barren Sahel region – which for years had been suffering from severe drought – productive and livable again.

At the time no one could have known that this concert would be the beginning both of a large-scale reforestation project in the Sahel region and of my future company, André Rieu Productions, Inc.

In good spirits, but completely inexperienced in this field, the members of the committee, Marjorie, and I began to organise what quickly took on the name of Gala Concert. Until then I had never organised a concert myself. The Maastricht Salon Orchestra was usually hired by

---

[9] Niou is a state and city in Burkina Faso.

theatres or businesses to play for a pre-arranged fee, and there was still no talk at all of starting our own business.

Right from the start I wanted to make this a really big event, which meant engaging not only The Maastricht Salon Orchestra, but also choirs and soloists. I also thought that the concert hall where we still held the Hieringebiete Concert was much too small. We had to find a larger hall that could accommodate many more people, because the larger the audience, the higher the proceeds, and the bigger the donation to the good cause.

Despite my inexperience, I took complete charge of the artistic organisation. I succeeded in engaging a number of well-known artists: the Maastreechter Staar (a well-known men's choir in the Netherlands), the sopranos Marjon Lambriks and Ans Humblet, Ger Withag's children's choir, and last but not least, The Maastricht Salon Orchestra itself. Everyone we invited was enthusiastic about the idea and accepted wholeheartedly. Not only the artists, but the local authorities and all the other people we approached also offered their help free of charge. I thought it truly fantastic! The Eurohal, at that time the largest hall in Maastricht, was also put at our disposal at no cost.

It was not only the organisation that was important; it was crucial to have good publicity as well. Marjorie wrote press releases and sent out photographs, while I gave interviews to newspapers and radio stations to make the concert and its good cause known to as wide a public as possible, also on the other side of the Dutch border. While I was being interviewed on a Belgian radio program, there was a telephone call from a secretary at the university of Ghent. She was delighted with our plan and asked us to get in touch as soon as possible with her boss, a certain Professor Van Cotthem. This I did, and learned that his faculty (plant genealogy) was working toward the same goal, namely, planting trees in barren areas. Professor Van Cotthem was very interested in our story and promised to come to Maastricht in the near future to discuss things in more detail. His visit resulted not only in intensive and continued collaboration between our committee and the university of Ghent, but also in our forming a close friendship with this likeable fellow.

We were extremely happy to have the help of
Willem van Cotthem, an expert in his field,
who made a discovery of immense importance
in the fight against deforestation and desertification.
He invented a mixture of so-called polymers,
synthetic granules, and certain fertilizers.
To put it simply, this mixture, called terracottem,
is put into the ground around young
trees shortly before the rainy season.
The granules then soak up water, retain it for months
if necessary, and subsequently release it
very slowly into the ground, giving it to the roots
of the trees and enabling them to survive the long, dry period
and to continue growing normally. In this way it
should be possible to turn a whole desert green again.

I found Professor van Cotthem's discovery so fascinating that it made me even more determined to go on with our plans. So besides organising the concert, we launched a campaign on the radio encouraging businesses to fund the planting of extra trees in the Sahel region.

To tell you the truth, we'd actually bitten off a bit more than we could chew, and the organisation of the Gala Concert turned into a race against the clock. It seemed as though everything would be ready in time, however. A total of 1600 tickets had been sold for the concert, a number that we'd hardly dared hope for. After all, in those days I wasn't so well known as I am now! The rehearsals had gone well, the program was full of surprises, the VIPs we'd asked to come, including representatives of environmental protection organisations, had all accepted our invitation, and everything seemed set. Radio Limburg would broadcast the concert live, so that the listeners at home could phone in and make pledges to plant trees as well.

On the day of the concert, however, everyone was suddenly in a state of panic! The rumour had swiftly spread (though no one knew where it started) that Marjon Lambriks wouldn't be able to make it!

What a catastrophe! Now what? She was the star of the evening and if she didn't show up the audience would be sorely disappointed. The whole program threatened to fall through: La Lambriks was supposed to sing a number with the men's choir, another with the children's choir, and a duet with the soprano Ans Humblet. What would we do without

The Gala Concert with, among others, Marjon Lambriks and the men's choir, the Mastreechter Staar. The proceeds of this concert went to the fund set up to 'Save the Sahel Region', but that wasn't the only thing that made this a special concert. It was also of tremendous importance for my career.

her? I couldn't conjure up another program so quickly. To make matters worse, during the dress rehearsal in the afternoon the sound system appeared to produce a terrible noise. It was really too awful to listen to! Even though the experts assured me that it would sound perfect in the evening in a hall filled with people, I didn't trust it for a second. My nerves began to act up and I broke out in a cold sweat. A huge flower arrangement that was supposed to hang above the stage was delivered, and we saw that it had been made in the shape of a giant cross, not exactly suitable for a festive Gala Concert. One of my sons saw it lying in the hallway and asked inquisitively, 'Papa, is this actually a funeral?'

As a result of everything that was threatening to go wrong at the last minute, I was in such a state of nervous exhaustion right before the concert that I apparently said something like, 'They can take their trees and shove them up their a-!' (I'm not usually given to uttering such vulgarities, I hasten to add! Things got to be so nerve-racking that it just slipped out.) The committee continues to tease me about it to this day.

Anyway, to make a long story short, Marjon Lambriks showed up after all and she sang beautifully, as did all the others. The flower arrangement was modified to suit the occasion, the sound system was working perfectly that evening, and all the other problems seemed to solve themselves as well. The Gala Concert for the Sahel region on that memorable 20 June 1987 was such a success that people in Maastricht were still talking about it years later. The proceeds were more than 40,000 guilders (then about £12,140), an amount that neither the committee nor I had dreamed possible.

A couple of months later Sjef Vink and Professor van Cotthem left for Burkina Faso, along with a team from the university of Ghent, to plant 'our' forest with their own hands. Initially it was a forest of 5000 trees and it was baptized the Bois de L'amité Maastricht-Niou (Forest of Friendship between Maastricht and Niou). Naturally we are extremely proud of having accomplished this with our music. The trees that were planted then have meanwhile reached a height of five to six metres. Their main purpose is to make the ground in that barren area fertile again, so that vegetable plots can be planted between the trees.

Since that Gala Concert we have continued to devote ourselves to saving the Sahel region. Marjorie joined the committee and served for years as secretary. Although thousands of trees have been added to the friendship forest over the years, money is still needed to continue our fight against desertification and deforestation, which is why I'll definitely be giving another benefit concert for the Sahel region sometime soon.

BAD LUCK!

*F*or years the '*Serenade* with the Nightingale' mentioned earlier and the Hieringebiete Concert every year on Ash Wednesday were the two pillars on which the success of The Maastricht Salon Orchestra rested. The record of the *Serenade*, which was played continually on Belgian radio, had done a lot to enhance our reputation, and the Hieringebiete Concert was known far beyond the borders of the province of Limburg, thanks to the live radio broadcast every year. This concert on Ash Wednesday, whose atmosphere is reminiscent of London's 'The Last Night of the Proms', became a new tradition in Maastricht, just as inextricably wrapped up with Carnival as the big parade on Carnival Sunday.[10]

Throughout these years the program consisted entirely of pieces that belonged to the standard repertoire of The Maastricht Salon Orchestra. Except for the traditional song *Am Aschermittwoch ist alles vorbei (It's all over on Ash Wednesday)*, we never felt tempted to play real Carnival music. After all, Carnival is over by Ash Wednesday, and it is just such wonderful, moving waltzes and well-known operetta melodies by composers such as Franz Lehár and Emmerich Kálmán that ease the transition from the excitement of Carnival back to the humdrum of everyday life. We did however perform a more or less Carnivalesque act each year, which we all thought up together, all of us being the members of The Maastricht Salon Orchestra and Marjorie. We always had a tremendous amount of fun doing this. Over the years many well-known people took part in these acts, including the men's choir known as the Mastreechter Staar, the television commentator Huub Mans, the actor and artist Pieke Dassen, and the tenor Wim Steinbusch.

It would be going too far to describe all eighteen Hieringebiete Concerts, although they were all high points in the career of The Maastricht Salon Orchestra. A couple of them, however, really were extra special, such as that one, in 1990, that was supposed to take place outside, on

[10] As mentioned in earlier chapters, Carnival is Maastricht's version of Mardi Gras.

Maastricht's market place. The theatre and the concert hall had been too small for a long time, the much larger Eurohal was no longer in use, and the MECC, Maastricht's new convention centre, located on the edge of the city, was still too far away for many died-in-the-wool 'Maastrichtenaren'. I had therefore taken the initiative to approach the local authorities and apply for permission to set up for one day only a huge tent in the middle of town, on the market place, for the purpose of staging the Hieringebiete Concert.

Months of preparation were necessary to get the act off the ground. There were endless talks with the local authorities, the fire department, the 'market master,' tent builders, technical personnel, you name it. But it came off. Everything, the whole scenario for Tuesday night (setting up the tent) and Wednesday, was ready on time, and everyone was lined up for the start.

This was still before Carnival had started, mind you, because from Sunday through Tuesday you can't do anything in Maastricht except celebrate Carnival. You certainly can't trouble anyone with organisational problems, or, for that matter, with any other kind of problem.

It was the Friday before Carnival, a beautiful, sunny, spring day, which held promises of a fantastic three-day celebration. Marjorie sat in her little office upstairs, listening to the weather forecast as announced by the famous – one might almost say 'lyrical' – 'king of the weather' of Belgian radio, Armand Pien. There was supposedly bad weather on the way, a storm the likes of which hadn't been seen for years! Armand's voice even took on a threatening tone as he warned his listeners to be as cautious as possible: 'Dear people, please stay at home. Don't go out if it's not absolutely necessary, because it will be disastrous, especially by the middle of next week, when the storm reaches its peak!'

Marjorie didn't listen to the rest of the forecast. She ran downstairs to bring me the bad news. By the middle of next week, on Wednesday of all days! Panic! Should we believe the weatherman? It was such beautiful weather, it couldn't change just like that. We phoned other weather stations, this time in the Netherlands, and they were less pessimistic. True, there were going to be strong winds, but a severe storm? It probably wouldn't be so bad, they told me, I shouldn't get so upset about it.

But what should we do? There wasn't much time. It was Friday afternoon, in a couple of hours the working week would be over and all of Maastricht would be in the grips of Carnival. Organising something else would mean an all-out effort, but whatever I decided to do, I'd have to do it fast. It was impossible, when you thought about it, ridiculous even to try. On the other hand, could I run the risk next Wednesday of having thousands of people flock to a tent that might collapse in a storm?

I'm not sure what it was that caused me to make up my mind. Perhaps it was a feeling of loyalty to the Belgians, who had been such faithful fans of mine all these years. I decided to believe Armand Pien and cancelled the tent. And it was a good thing I did, because that Wednesday the weather was catastrophic. A terrible storm swept the whole country, and even the Eurohal, where we'd arranged to play at the last minute, was barely left standing. During the concert part of the roof caved in, though luckily not in the hall where the concert was taking place. After the concert there was a moment of panic when people began surging toward the exit, only to find their way blocked by those already at the door who were afraid to set foot in that terrible weather.

Nothing worse happened, though, and we were thankful for that. It turned out to be a wonderful concert, and I eventually recovered financially from the losses I'd incurred in cancelling the tent.

I doubt if I'll ever organise another concert in a tent. One thing I know for sure, and that is that Armand Pien's legendary reputation is not based solely on legend!

The year after that was the thirteenth (!) Hieringebiete Concert. I'm not at all superstitious, and unlike many others who had become wary after the previous year's experience, I was looking forward to the concert. For no good reason, it turned out, because our bad luck in 1990 was nothing compared with what was about to happen.

It was January 1991 and Carnival was slowly approaching. As usual, the Hieringebiete Concert had been planned down to the last detail, thousands of tickets had been sold, and everyone was looking forward to the enjoyable event.

But suddenly those ominous, big black headlines appeared on the front page of every newspaper: WAR! Everyone's worst fears had come true – war had broken out in Kuwait, occupied by Saddam Hussein. The world reacted with fear and misgiving. The German government called off the upcoming Carnival celebrations and the Netherlands quickly followed suit. All of the festivities associated with Carnival – parades, the crowning of 'Prince Carnival', costume balls – were cancelled and the princes of the various cities were sent home. The year 1991 was doomed to be a year without Carnival.

Now what? The Hieringebiete Concert was not, strictly speaking, part of Carnival, but still ... Could we unthinkingly go ahead with our concert? Would it be appropriate to play such happy, exuberant music under such circumstances? Perhaps we ought to turn it into an altogether more sober affair, a sort of requiem for those who had already died in the Gulf War. Our public didn't expect this kind of music from us, though. I had no idea what to do. On the one hand, just like many other people in the world, we felt threatened and were in no mood to celebrate. On the other hand, I felt it was my duty to cheer people up in these difficult times, and I felt really sorry for the thousands of people who had been looking forward to the concert for so long. We couldn't decide what to do.

That is, not until I turned on the television and saw the impassioned speech given by the mayor of Tel Aviv, who made a valiant attempt to boost the spirits of the terrified inhabitants of his city. 'Enjoy life for as long as you can,' I heard him say, 'sing and dance and have fun!'

His words decided the matter for me: I wouldn't disappoint my public. We would play the concert, just as we'd planned it, and give the people the chance to relax and forget the threat of war, at least for those few hours.

And sure enough, that is what happened. Perhaps because of the tenseness and anxiety everyone was feeling, there was a fantastic atmosphere during the concert. The proceeds went to Unicef for their action to help the children in the Gulf, and afterwards I was both glad and grateful that I'd decided to give the concert after all.

After that there were no more catastrophes to hinder the Hieringebiete Concert. We gave the concert with great pleasure for eighteen years, also in a number of other towns. Thanks to the record of the same name that was recorded live in 1989 and had meanwhile earned a Gold Record, the Hieringebiete Concert became known throughout the country, even though I still have the impression that outsiders don't really understand the meaning of this funny word!

PART THREE

$\mathcal{T}$HE JOHANN STRAUSS ORCHESTRA

THE JOHANN STRAUSS ORCHESTRA:

VIOLIN
Kremi Mineva
Frank Steijns
Jet Gelens
Lin Jong
Diana Morsinkhof
Freya Cremers
Els Mercken
Boris Goldenblank
Lara Meuleman
Vincenzo Viola
Giedre Mundinaite
Gosia Loboda
Cord Meyer
Agnes Fizzano
Jennifer Haas

VIOLA
Linda Custers
Klaartje Polman
Nadejda Diakoff

CELLO
Tanja Derwahl
Margriet van Lexmond
Hanneke Roggen
Karin Hinze
Joëlle Tonnaer

DOUBLE BASS
Roland Lafosse
Franco Vulcano
Jean Sassen

FLUTE/PICCOLO
Teun Ramaekers
Nathalie Bolle

OBOE
Arthur Cordewener

CLARINET
Manoe Konings

SAXOPHONE/
BASSOON
Sanne Mestrom

TRUMPET
Roger Diederen
René Henket

HORN
Noël Perdaens

TROMBONE
Ruud Merx
Leon van Wijk

BASS TUBA
Ton Maessen

PIANO
Stéphanie Detry

HARP
Vera Kool

SYNTHESIZER
Ward Vlasveld

PERCUSSION &
TIMPANY
Marcel Falize
Mireille Brepols
Glenn Falize

CHOIR
Karin Haine
Virgenie Henket
Judith Luesink
Anna Reker
Kalki Schrijvers
Nicolle Steins

HELP,
I'M A VIOLINIST!

I've already written that 20 June 1987 was a special day for me. That day and the events preceding it brought about a great change in my career. For me the Gala Concert on behalf of the Sahel region actually meant the beginning of a completely new type of career, that of entrepreneur – not yet in the legal sense of the word, though that came later as a matter of course. That concert had been the very first concert in which we had taken the initiative, in other words, the first one that we had organised completely on our own, albeit with the help of the Maastricht-Niou committee members.

We had done it all ourselves single-handedly, without having a contract with a theatre, and without anyone else bearing any of the responsibility for the financial risks involved. Admittedly, the risks were smaller for a benefit concert than they would have been for a normal concert, because of all the people who offered their services free of charge. Still, it had been a tough job and we'd managed it completely on our own, and the fact that it had been a success boosted my self-confidence.

I was determined to start organising more things myself. The idea of having a goal in mind and striving to achieve it appealed to me, especially since I now enjoyed the prospect of being able to bring it off as successfully as the Gala Concert. Best of all I liked the idea of being completely independent, of not having a boss to tell me what I could or couldn't do, which pieces I should or shouldn't play, and from when to when I had to rehearse.

Thanks to the success of that first concert 'of my own', I dared to venture out a while later – though naturally in consultation with Marjorie – to produce my own concerts and to take the inevitable financial risks. Who knows, maybe some day we'd succeed in starting our own business!

Oddly enough, this is something that people often reproach me for, perhaps because such behaviour is exceptional in a musician. Conservatories of music train musicians to play their instruments and try to instill in them a general knowledge of music. They're barely concerned with teaching incipient musicians how to earn a living, which is surely one of the most important aspects of it all! Unfortunately, this part of their training is neglected completely. Earning money making music is something that is rarely mentioned in the Dutch world of (subsidised!) classical music. It's a distasteful subject and beneath your dignity to talk about it. This is a strange and also pitiable situation. You practice for years and years – maybe an average of eighteen, if you consider that many children start to play a musical instrument around the age of five or six – to reach an acceptable standard. But you're not at all aware at the time that you'll have to earn a living playing that instrument of yours. Like practically all music students, during your long years of study you dream of a career as a famous soloist, even though you know that only a few ever achieve this. Then you finally get your degree and realise that no one has asked you to tour the world giving solo concerts – this is the fate of 99 percent of all music students – and there you are, inexperienced and at loose ends. You take a good look round and think, 'Help, I'm a violinist, now what?' This is what happened to me at the beginning. I eventually learned the hard way and became more and more determined to take things into my own hands.

Part of my decision, of course, was also due to Marjorie's influence, who encouraged me to become a proper 'businessman'. She had an academic background herself, though she came from a family of businessmen, people who had earned her lifelong respect by having to fight hard to make a living.

Besides the fact that she was eager to learn, doing business had always been in her blood. While still a little girl, she had taken great pleasure in combining 'business' and 'scholarship'! When she was eight she made covers for her rather extensive collection of children's books, put labels on them bearing the title, author's name, and age group for which they were suitable, and lent them out to children in the neighbourhood for two cents apiece. Always the meticulous one, she kept a record of all the books lent out in a special notebook, and her library was a huge success.

That the combination of 'business' and 'the arts' had also appealed to her from an early age is apparent from the fact that, when she was ten years old and had been taking ballet lessons for several years, she turned her room into a ballet studio. The edge of her foldaway bed served as the exercise bar. Still just a little girl herself but brimming with precocious enthusiasm, she gave ballet lessons for ten cents an hour to her young friends.

In the years following there was not much time for experimenting in the business sector. It eventually became apparent that her interests lay elsewhere. She devoted herself to her studies and became a teacher of German and Italian at a high school in Maastricht, as well as a research assistant at the university of Nijmegen. The faculty's personnel policy at that time meant that as a woman she had no hope of getting a permanent job (luckily things have changed a lot since then), so she decided to devote her time and energy to one of her favourite hobbies – translating books. Her free time was mostly given up to music and dance, school cabaret, and student drama groups, whereby she not only acted in the plays, but also helped to organise the productions.

When, in the first days of The Maastricht Salon Orchestra, I mentioned to Marjorie that I was looking for someone to manage the business side of things for me, she offered to do it on a temporary basis, because she had no translating job at the time. In any case she thought she could help me out until I'd found someone else to do it, thinking she could spare about four or five weeks, which was the usual length of time between completing one translation and receiving an offer for the next one.

She found her new work so fascinating, however, that the 'little businesswoman' she'd been as a child seemed to wake up again. She became more and more involved with The Maastricht Salon Orchestra, broadened her knowledge of music and entertainment, and after a while no longer had any time for translating. The weeks turned into months, then years, then decades! Marjorie has been my manager now for thirty-six years. For more than fifteen years she took responsibility for the entire organisation: obtaining engagements, negotiating with theatre managers and businesses, making appointments, overseeing the finances, taking care of publicity, and carrying out general office duties.

She's always done her work with the utmost pleasure. It's no wonder, then, that after spending so many years in the company of my manager-wife, I've also acquired a taste for organisation and entrepreneurship.

STRAUSS?
NO, THANK YOU!

$\mathscr{A}$long time before I got the urge to start my own business, another idea had taken hold of me. After having performed with The Maastricht Salon Orchestra for seven or eight years, I was beginning to feel that I wanted more. Perhaps a larger orchestra, or different music. I wasn't sure exactly. I got a lot of pleasure from the salon orchestra, it's true, both from playing together with my colleagues and from the repertoire. Slowly but surely, though, something else had begun brewing in my mind. I began putting different ensembles together on paper, most of them consisting of strings, because that's the sound I like the best. My father was still alive at the time, and together we carefully studied the repertoire that the various ensembles would be able to play. Luckily I saved the handwritten list that he drew up for me, and now that he's dead, it represents one of my last, dear memories of him. Included in this list were the splendid adagios by Albinoni and Barber, Britten's *Simple Symphony,* Concerti Grossi by Corelli and Handel, and many more beautiful pieces that I intend to perform someday with my orchestra. At the time, though, I wasn't sure whether this kind of music, no matter how beautiful, was the kind of music I really wanted to play for my public.

For months I was in a quandary: on the one hand, this beautiful music really appealed to me; on the other hand, I didn't want to give up the wonderful atmosphere of those concerts with The Maastricht Salon Orchestra. And I didn't need anyone to tell me that an 'Albinoni Evening' was anything but fun! In the early days of the salon orchestra, we had once played a purely classical program, by way of experiment. We played well-known pieces, such as Schubert's *Military March*, minuets by Boccherini and Beethoven, the *Serenade* by Haydn, and the *Air* by Bach, each and every one a gem. Normally we play one or two of these pieces in any given concert, and they are always greatly appreciated by the audience. But at that one concert of only 'serious' music, the audience, who was used to hearing us play the *Skaters Waltz* and *Plaisir d'amour*, didn't know what had hit them, and neither did we! Our usual relaxed atmosphere was nowhere to be found, there was nothing to laugh about, and all five of us got clammy hands from the ordeal. I can still hear the double bass player, Jean, who said during the intermission, 'Say, André, shouldn't we just go back out there and play *Susie*?'

What I now had in mind was something just as entertaining as a typical evening with The Maastricht Salon Orchestra, but with a larger orchestra and a more extensive repertoire. The stories I told between numbers would remain part of it too, as I could no longer imagine a concert without talking to the audience. At that time I still hadn't given any thought to making stage sets and costumes and putting on a show.

These vague plans had occupied my thoughts for quite some time already, and I'd been forming ensembles on paper, searching for new repertoire, and asking colleagues if they felt like working with me, when suddenly another happy coincidence occurred that helped to point me in the right direction.

———

Besides all the hard work and long hours I've put in, a couple of lucky things have happened to me that have also contributed to my success. Sometimes you just have to be lucky, although I'm convinced that you can actually attract luck. Someone once wrote in a 'wish book' for one of our children, 'Look to the sun, then the shadows will fall behind you,' and that is exactly what I strive for, to look at the bright side of life. I'm generally optimistic and always assume that everything will eventually turn out all right. I believe in the positive power in each person, including myself, and think that this is the reason for my success. I've never just sat at home, expecting 'happiness' or 'success' to fall in my lap, and moaning if it didn't. I've always gone out to try my luck for myself, in the firm conviction that something good would happen. And usually something did. (By the way, I found that 'wish book' a great idea. When our children were born, Marjorie had everyone who came to visit us write a wish for the new-born baby in a book. We kept their 'wish books' in a safe place, so that when our boys left home they could take their 'book' with them as they made their own way in the world. We all look at them once in a while and enjoy reading the amusing remarks and words of wisdom written by many of our friends, relatives, and colleagues. They are unique and precious possessions, the more so because many of the 'authors' are no longer alive.)

———

As I started to say before, while I was searching for a new form for my group, something happened to put me on the right track, although this wasn't immediately apparent at the time. After a concert in the Wijngracht Theatre in Kerkrade, the manager, Matthew Schmeitz, the previously mentioned 'godfather' of The Maastricht Salon Orchestra, came up to me. He is a very active theatre manager and travels around the world searching for foreign productions that are also interesting for Dutch audiences.

During one of his trips to London he had met an English producer who organised successful 'Strauss Nights' with ballet, voice, and orchestra. Working together with that producer, Matthew wanted to get something similar started in the Netherlands. He asked me, 'Doesn't the idea appeal to you, André? You could form an orchestra and accompany that English ballet.' Although I could see that it would be a unique opportunity to start working at last with a larger orchestra, I said a heartfelt 'no'. With all respect to ballet, this was the last thing I wanted to do. I could just picture it all: singers and dancers wearing beautiful costumes on a stage with magnificent scenery, and my orchestra and I down below in the pit, shrouded in darkness and practically invisible, with my back to the audience to boot. The pit was the pits, as far as I was concerned. People who aren't habitual opera-goers sometimes ask themselves who that fellow is who suddenly appears on stage to take a bow at the end of the performance. It's the conductor! You can't blame them for not knowing who he is, especially as they haven't seen anything but his back the whole evening.

The thing that I found most disconcerting about Matthew's plan to accompany a ballet was the idea of always having to play in a strict, measured tempo, without any rubato[11] or ritardando,[12] because otherwise you can't dance to the music. And it's precisely this freedom of expression that makes music so interesting and exciting, both for the musicians and the audience.

Matthew's suggestion continued to haunt me, however. Strauss's music was marvellous, I had always admired his waltzes and regretted not being able to play them with The Maastricht Salon Orchestra, which was only five people strong. That Viennese atmosphere, full of romance and elegance, also fit in with the picture I had of my new orchestra. But accompanying singers and dancers the whole evening? No, no, a thousand times no! I couldn't bring myself to do it, the violinist and soloist in me forbade it.

---

[11] Literally 'stolen' time, to be played with a flexible tempo.
[12] Becoming slower.

I continued to think about it, though. I talked it over with Marjorie, and slowly but surely the various bits and pieces coalesced into a concrete picture of the type of performance I wanted to give. I decided to accept Matthew's proposal, but only on certain conditions. There would be no English 'Strauss Night' with singers and ballet dancers on stage, accompanied by an orchestra in the pit. It would be a Viennese evening that was first and foremost a concert, in that the orchestra would be the main attraction. The ballet would have only a subordinate role.

Here Marjorie had just cut my hair (which she still does!). I remember the afternoon she was cutting my hair and was continually interrupted by the telephone ringing. Finally she'd had enough of constantly having to put down the scissors and talk to clients. When the phone rang again, she picked up the receiver and said crossly, 'Rieu Hairdressers!' On the other end of the line was a producer from Belgian Radio and Television...

'Darn, a lost opportunity,' flashed into Marjorie's mind, but it was someone putting together a special program and looking for a group that was actually not a professional ensemble. They wanted someone who made music in addition to having a real (!) job. If Mr Rieu ran a hairdresser's and had a salon orchestra on the side, then that was just what they were looking for. Sometimes you just have to be lucky!

Actually I'm not fond of theatres.
As the true son of a symphony conductor,
I like concert halls much more. I've felt at home in them
since I was a child. Their acoustics are more to my liking,
there are no annoying curtains and wings,
and most importantly, they lend themselves more to
the kind of atmosphere I want to create during my concerts.
What happens on stage is real and honest;
it's not just a show, not just an illusion that's over
and done with as soon as the curtain falls.
In a concert hall I feel closer to the audience than in a theatre.
In theatres it's customary to dim the lights
before the play or opera begins, whereas in concert
halls the lights are traditionally kept on, enabling me
to see my audience, which is very important to me.
I want to be able to look at people properly,
to see the expressions on their faces.
I want to see whether they're laughing or crying, and
whether they're enjoying the music. Only in this way can
I establish any contact with my audience
and spark off their participation. In a theatre
everything is different: there are wings that spoil
the acoustics, to begin with, and all kinds of things
happen there which distract the musicians.
Moreover, there is a curtain that has to rise and fall,
and lights in the hall that seem to need dimming.
I've had an ongoing battle with stage managers and
other experts in the field for as long as I've been
organising my own concerts. I want the lights to
stay on in the hall, and no curtain, not before
the concert, or in the intermission, or afterwards.
I want to be able to decide for myself when
a concert is finished, and this is a decision you
make together with your audience. You feel
when the concert should finish, when the time has come
to give no more encores, no matter how much fun everyone is having.
A closed curtain seems so definite and commanding, you might as well
make an announcement, such as
'You might as well go home now, ladies and gentlemen,
there's nothing else to see, it's all over.'

It's difficult to get your way about this in a theatre:
there's a curtain, so it has to fall, and there are lights,
so they have to be turned off. Nonsense, as far as
I'm concerned. Usually my battle with the stage
manager ends in a compromise, because I'm also
receptive to what the people sitting in the hall have to say.
Marjorie is not alone in thinking that it's equally exciting
to experience a closed curtain, lights that are suddenly
dimmed, the buzzing crowd falling silent, and then
the curtain rising, and the surprise of seeing the set
for the first time. Moreover, the Netherlands is not
at all blessed with good concert halls, so I can do nothing but try to
make the best of the situation when we play in theatres.

———————————

Technical problems of this kind arose during the very first production, though these were not the only obstacles to be overcome before the English 'Strauss Night' was transformed into a Dutch 'Viennese Evening'.

The first problem was the fact that I didn't want to play only Strauss the whole evening long. There was so much other beautiful Viennese music that deserved to be played, music that I thought shouldn't be missing from such an evening, such as the immortal operetta melodies by Kálmán, Lehár, and Stolz, and all those well-known Viennese songs like Mei Mutterl war a Weanerin ('My Mother was Viennese'), Heut kommen d'Engerln auf Urlaub nach Wien ('Today the angels come on holiday to Vienna'), or the moving Fiakerlied ('Vienna Coachman's Song').[13] I was convinced that my audiences would enjoy them, and that's what they came for, after all, to enjoy themselves. I thought this music was wonderful and had the feeling I'd be able to put together a marvellous program using it all.

For a moment I'd forgotten the Englishman, however, that clever producer from London who had thought up the 'Strauss Night' in the first place. He was completely beside himself when Matthew, Marjorie, and I arrived in London to announce our plans to modify his program. 'Strauss, Strauss, and more Strauss' was his motto, 'ten pieces before the intermission and ten pieces afterwards, and nothing else!'

Luckily Matthew proved to be our staunch ally, and together the three of us were able to persuade him that his English 'Night' wouldn't be such a hit with my Dutch audience. It wasn't that people didn't

[13] A Fiaker is a Viennese two-horse carriage.

appreciate Strauss in the Netherlands, but I didn't feel like playing Strauss and nothing but Strauss the whole evening. I knew that if we did I wouldn't be able to achieve what I wanted and what the people expected of me, which was providing them with an evening of relaxation, letting them laugh at jokes and humorous sketches, touching their hearts with romantic melodies, and then sending them home, happy and content. In order to do this, variety is of the utmost importance.

The poor Englishman gave in, not for the last time. Most of all he regretted that this Dutch production would not be an evening of pure ballet – English ballet, surely that was heaven on earth!

It is perhaps important to point out that the English have a great tradition in ballet and that ballet dancers are highly respected by the general public. The English have some of the best ballet schools in the world, and ballet performances in England are generally of exceptionally high quality. The producer had therefore wanted the dancers on stage in front, with me and my 'band' at the back, preferably hidden behind a gauze curtain, so that nothing would distract the attention of the public from the dancers.

If the Englishman had had his way, I would have had no choice but to say, 'Never! Goodbye, sir, nice to have met you!' Then there would be no Viennese evening in the Netherlands, at least not with me. How could I have any contact with the audience from the back of the stage? They wouldn't even be able to see me! Putting the orchestra in front of the dancers wouldn't work either, because then you could only see the dancers' heads, and that wouldn't be very exciting. It seemed to be an insurmountable problem.

Not for me, though. I suddenly had a brilliant idea, at least so it seemed to me. I've already told you about my obsession with technology. According to Marjorie, I'll go to ridiculous extremes to prove that you can do almost anything with modern technology. I therefore invented a sort of rolling riser, a platform on wheels on which the orchestra could sit and let themselves be rolled forward when there were no dancers on stage, and pulled backwards whenever the ballet made an appearance. What I would have liked most was to operate it myself from a remote control switch attached to my violin! (A ridiculous idea? Not at all!) The riser, rigged up to be pulled backwards by means of cables and pushed forward by poles, would be manoeuvred around by stagehands stationed behind the backdrop. Like this I would be able to play the concerts in my 'normal' manner, at the front of the stage, face to face with the audience, yielding the stage once in a while to the dancers. We all thought it a nice compromise. (In practice things didn't work out quite as I had expected, but I'll tell you more about that later.)

Altogether the talks in London lasted for three days. After much wrangling we were finally able to agree about the basic content and form of the program, and I decided to give it a try. It became an Anglo-Dutch co-production, whereby I was responsible for the program and the orchestra, and the producer in London would 'deliver' the singer and dancers. The new project would be launched under the name of *Wien Bleibt Wien (Vienna Forever)*.

POVERTY, COLD, AND
THREE-FOUR TIME

*E*ven before Matthew Schmeitz had approached me with the suggestion for the Strauss evening, I had already found a number of musicians who were prepared to work with me on something new and were willing to take a leap in the dark. After all, that's what it was. What did I have to offer them? Nothing at all! I wanted to form a larger orchestra and try out the new sound, that was all for the time being. I still didn't know what exactly we were going to play, and we didn't have any firm engagements to look forward to. I had assured them, however, that something would come of it. Thanks to the reputation of The Maastricht Salon Orchestra, they had so much faith in me that they were willing to give it a try.

After returning from London I could finally start rehearsing a definite program. I didn't have a rehearsal hall for this larger group of musicians – we had usually held the rehearsals for The Maastricht Salon Orchestra in one of our homes – and there was no money to rent a place. I was therefore at the mercy of other people's goodwill.

Because it was nearly Christmas and the schools would be closed for two weeks of holiday, I received permission to rehearse for two weeks in the neighbourhood school that our children attended. The only snag was that they didn't heat it during holidays. No problem, I thought, I would take care of that with a couple of electric heaters. This was before I knew how cold those last, dark days of the year would be!

During that Christmas holiday I walked to school in the cold at six o'clock every morning to turn on the electric heaters, so that the ice-cold room would be warm enough to start rehearsing at nine o'clock. The hot soup that Marjorie brought during the break kept us going somehow, warming our fingers up just enough to play.

This did not hold true for everyone, however, because after the first half-hour, a violinist got up and announced that in any case he wasn't crazy enough to sit there playing in three-four time in the freezing cold. (I don't know what he found worse, the cold or the three-four time!) He walked out, and for a minute I was afraid that before long everyone else would follow suit.

I couldn't really blame him, could I? Was it right of me to expect people to give of themselves completely and rehearse with me for at least half a year in order to build up our repertoire, with only the prospect of a short tour that wouldn't take place for another year? The theatres plan their seasons at least that far in advance. And would Marjorie be able to sell concerts by this new ensemble that didn't even have a name yet? Would I earn enough money to pay them? Wasn't this just some hare-brained scheme that would come to nothing?

There were enough times that I was so discouraged I wanted to give up. But 'giving up' is a notion quite foreign to me, and deep down inside I was convinced that all this drudgery would lead to something good in the end. So I stuck to my guns and tried not to worry about people leaving. I would always find someone to replace them. Luckily most of the musicians remained enthusiastic, as witnessed by the existence now of a hardcore of musicians who started out with me more than twenty-five years ago.

One of the biggest problems facing me was a chronic shortage of time. There was almost no opportunity to do anything else alongside my concerts with The Maastricht Salon Orchestra and my job with The Limburg Symphony Orchestra. Besides the morning rehearsals, about four evenings a week were taken up by the orchestra as well. To complicate matters, the dates of our concerts and occasional evening rehearsals were not always known a long time in advance, making it difficult for Marjorie to accept firm engagements for my new orchestra. There could be no question of a tour of several weeks' length.

The best solution was obviously to give up my permanent job with The Limburg Symphony Orchestra. But simply quitting ... well, that wasn't something that you did without giving it a great deal of thought. Fortunately, the opportunity of working only part-time presented itself a short while later, which gave me a bit of leeway as far as juggling my schedule was concerned. My co-principal in the second violin section was a nice colleague who was sympathetic to my work outside the orchestra, and after consulting him I could more or less decide which days I wanted to be free. That half-time job meant, of course, only half of an already meager salary! If I ever wanted to be an independent musician, however, then there was nothing to do but take the risk. Luckily Marjorie supported me one hundred percent. We both had the feeling that, with a certain amount of effort, it must be possible to get by on half my former salary. (Two years later, on the evening before my fortieth birthday, I would quit the orchestra completely.)

Now, after so many years, I sometimes ask myself where I got the nerve to take such risks. After all, I was responsible for supporting my wife and two children and paying the mortgage on our house. It's not as though I've ever regretted anything I've done – on the contrary! – but at that time it was like setting sail without a compass. Way back then I had no idea whatsoever that my wild plans would eventually have such successful results. Things might just as easily have turned out badly, for all I knew!

What drove me on, I think, was the great pleasure I took in the music I played, all those moving melodies that make so many people happy. It was the same enthusiasm that I'd had as a little boy when I'd started some new project or other. I would become obsessed with it and forget everything else around me, caught up in the spell of a new discovery. Appointments and duties no longer existed, only that one plan, that new go-cart I wanted to build, or that new idea I had for a cable-lift between our house and our neighbour's. As a child I could get so wrapped up in things that I completely forgot the world around me.

Once, when I was little, I passed a building site on the way to school where huge steam shovels were slowly driving back and forth, excavating a foundation. I'd never seen anything so wonderful, and I stood there watching, fascinated. When the other children came walking past again, this time in the opposite direction on their way home, I was astonished. I had lost all sense of time and had stood there the whole morning, completely forgetting to go to school!

It's just as well that I have the ability to forget everything around me. I'm quite capable of putting everything else out of my head and becoming totally absorbed in a concert or several hours of violin practice. And it's just as well that I have a wife who doesn't have this ability, otherwise things would always be going haywire around here!

The group I started rehearsing with was only twelve people strong, in my opinion still far from the ideal size. It was more than twice as big as the salon orchestra, though, so in any case I was able to expand our repertoire. I didn't dare hire more musicians, because in the end I'd have to be able to pay them all. I wasn't eligible for a government subsidy, as I wasn't doing anything 'innovative', and in those days sponsors simply weren't interested in me. After that first round of rehearsals in the elementary school, for which my only investment was renting a piano, paying the heating costs, and supplying soup and sandwiches, I was forced to rent a room in which we could rehearse at least once a week. This meant coughing up yet more money. Press releases, posters, and program booklets were printed, and I had to go to London to discuss things with the choreographer and to rehearse with the singer. To get this new ensemble off the ground, we had to invest all of our savings and then some, still with no guarantee that things would turn out all right.

We enjoyed it tremendously, however, both the challenge of doing something new and the wonderful Viennese music. For us that was the most important part, indeed the only thing that really mattered. No amount of money nor the security of a permanent job was worth as much as the happiness our work gave us.

Marjorie succeeded in booking a tour of fifteen concerts in the Netherlands, Belgium, and Germany. I laugh when I think back on it, because nowadays fifteen concerts a month seems like nothing. But in those days we thought it quite something, a real tour, and we were extremely proud of ourselves for having pulled it off.

After several try-outs the first tour finally started on 1 January 1988, with the orchestra that was baptized – how could it be otherwise? – The Johann Strauss Orchestra, after the composer who had actually brought it all about, the great man of three-four time, Johann Strauss, Jr himself.

IF ONLY I HAD A
MARKETABLE SKILL!

*O*nce again there were thrilling times in store for us: the excitement of a new orchestra and new repertoire, this time with ballet dancers and a singer as well. We'd had enough rehearsals, the orchestra knew all the music by heart, and the dress rehearsal with the singer and dancers had gone very well. But would I be up to it, the strain of a tour with fifteen concerts? It wasn't as though I had ever done it before. And what would we do if the singer fell ill during the tour, or one of the dancers broke a leg? But the all-important question was, of course, how would the audience react? And what would they be like? Would they be people who always came to concerts of The Maastricht Salon Orchestra, who had known me for a long time and were always prepared to laugh at my jokes? Or would these concerts attract a completely different kind of audience, fanatic opera-goers or ballet lovers, who would think that the orchestra shouldn't play so loud, and that that strange Stehgeiger[14] should keep his mouth shut?

Nerves, nerves, and more nerves ... And, as usual before going on stage, while waiting in the wings just before the premiere of *Vienna Forever* I blurted out, 'If only I had a marketable skill!'

That first tour – fifteen performances in January 1988, advertised by the theatres as a 'Festive New Year's Concert' – hardly resembles the concerts I give today. I'm shocked if I see photographs taken then! The twelve of us sat on the rolling riser I'd devised and spent a great deal of the evening at the back of the stage, barely visible to the audience. The members of The Johann Strauss Orchestra dressed in normal concert attire: the men in tails and the women in long black dresses. To tell you the truth, I hadn't stopped to give it much thought, or it might have occurred to me that a Viennese New Year's Concert should also be 'pleasing to the eye', as several critics rightly pointed out. Just as I'd

---

[14] A Stehgeiger is a violinist who stands at the front of the violin section, functioning as both concertmaster and conductor.

Vienna Forever (1988). If you look carefully you can see The Johann Strauss Orchestra (and even me!) somewhere back there in the dark!

always done with The Maastricht Salon Orchestra, I'd concentrated all my attention on the music and the remarks I'd prepared beforehand.

When the salon orchestra played, the five of us usually sat at the very front of the stage with a red or gold curtain behind us: four gentlemen in black, and, like a flower in their midst, the female cellist in a glittering evening dress. With a potted palm or two and nice lighting, it always presented a pretty picture. I had made a conscious choice not to devote too much attention to our outward appearance, thinking it only detracted from the music. It was up to us to evoke the right atmosphere with our music and my talking.

A 'Festive Viennese New Year's Concert', as described in the program books and by the press, was apparently something completely different. We hadn't given this any thought at all. Even if we had realised it, though, we wouldn't have had the money to do anything about it.

When I was asked by the theatre management what colour the masking should be,[15] I had answered, 'Black is fine.' It shows how much I knew! I had no idea that the backdrop would also be black, that the dancers who were coming from England would be wearing purple and black costumes, and that the singer would wear a dark blue dress that was barely distinguishable from black!

So when the curtain was raised on 1 January 1988 the audience caught its first glimpse of a scene which was more like a funeral parlour than a festive Viennese ballroom. Afterwards Marjorie told me that an acquaintance of hers, who was sitting in the row in front of her, turned around and asked cynically which convent I'd plundered for this décor. I didn't hear what Marjorie said in return, but I know that she usually answers such questions with a nonchalant shrug and a just-you-wait-and-see look.

And she turned out to be right! (Women are always right.) The sombre scene didn't dampen the audience's spirits in the slightest. Thanks to the magnificent music, the enthusiasm of the musicians and dancers, and the cheerful impression the orchestra made even then, the atmosphere during the premiere was one of festive exuberance.

Taking pleasure in playing together is really the most important thing in such an undertaking. The audience loves to see the musicians taking great pains to play together perfectly. You watch each other and the conductor, you know where the difficult passages are, and you sit in attention on the edge of your chair to make sure you play everything perfectly down to the last detail. And if you manage to get it right every time, making music like this is a source of tremendous enjoyment. Pure bliss! And the musicians radiate this pleasure to the audience. In addition to being skilled players and thoroughly professional musicians, willing to make every effort toward perfect ensemble playing, I require the people I hire to take great pleasure in precisely this kind of music, in other words, I never hire anyone who doesn't! The audience feels it instantly and can pick out anyone in the orchestra who isn't having fun. The musicians who audition for my orchestra don't have a chance if they don't meet this requirement. They may be musical geniuses and able to play like gods, but if they don't like 'my' kind of music, then I can't hire them. All those pieces by Strauss, Lehár, Kálmán, Stolz, and Offenbach are simply fantastic! They're overflowing with so much *joie de vivre* that they don't deserve to be played without enthusiasm. And because I keep very strictly to this rule, I always have an orchestra full of life and vigour.

This life and vigour was responsible for the huge success of the premiere of *Vienna Forever*. The tumultuous applause at the end and their calls for encores were sure signs that the audience had completely forgotten the sombre setting and had given themselves over to pure enjoyment.

The rest of that first tour was also a success. The concerts were nearly all sold out, the audiences were just as enthusiastic as those who came to hear the salon orchestra, and even the reviews were all very positive, with the exception of a few, not undeserved comments on the lack of an appropriate ambience.

All the theatres where we performed *Vienna Forever* booked us again for the following year and sometimes the year after that as well. Every year new venues were added until the annual tour gradually grew to include about fifty theatres in the Netherlands and Belgium.

The collaboration with the ballet, which had caused such headaches beforehand, actually turned out to be a lot of fun. They were all such nice people, those eight dancers whom we'd baptized The London Strauss Dancers, to go with The Johann Strauss Orchestra. They danced beautifully and my free tempos didn't give them any trouble at all.

The only real problem during this first tour was that invention of mine, the rolling riser. To prevent my orchestra from having to spend the whole evening at the back of the stage, I'd devised a system whereby the stagehands could roll us backwards and forwards 'invisibly' by means of iron cables and poles. Everyone had agreed beforehand that my invention wasn't such a bad idea.

What a nuisance it was in reality! Of the fifteen concerts there wasn't one where that stupid thing functioned like it was meant to. The wheels jammed and turned sideways, like those grocery-store trolleys that never go in the direction you want them to go. That riser rolled every which way except where it was supposed to. Sometimes it would only roll forward, but then at such a speed that we almost rolled right off the stage into the audience.

The worst was the performance in Roermond, in central Limburg. The concert was well underway, I had established a close rapport with the audience, and they were obviously enjoying themselves. I had just announced that we were about to play the splendid polka mazurka *Fata Morgana* by Johann Strauss, and had explained what a 'fata morgana' was – something you see that isn't really there. My last sentence – 'Ladies and gentlemen, you are about to see ... you won't believe your eyes ... applause, please, for The London Strauss Dancers!' – was the sign for the stage crew to pull our rolling riser backwards and make room for the dancers.

The audience applauded enthusiastically, but nothing happened. The riser stayed right where it was, and seemed to have no intention of moving, not forwards, not backwards, not right or left. The wheels had jammed completely. There was a deathly silence, both on the stage and in the hall. I tried to make a silly joke about a 'fata morgana', but there was hardly any laughter and the situation was getting downright painful. Stagehands came on to turn the wheels in the right direction, but nothing seemed to work. The only solution was to have the whole orchestra get off that stupid thing and wait at the side of the stage, holding their instruments, until the stagehands, with all the strength they could muster, succeeded in pushing it backwards. My embarrassment was indescribable!

When everything and everyone was in place and I was ready to play *Fata Morgana*, the whole audience started applauding wildly, with the exception of one concert-goer – Marjorie – who had apparently sunken into a hole in the floor.

The orchestra spent the rest of the evening, in suitable modesty, at the back of the stage, letting the dancers bask in the glory. And rightly so, I deserved nothing better. Technology is wonderful, but so unreliable.

All That Glitters
Is Not Gold

*I*n spite of the great success of that first tour, it was clear that some things had to be changed in the *Vienna Forever* production. In the first place I wanted to increase the size of the orchestra, so that its sound would be richer and more beautiful. Because we'd already been given a few more engagements for the following year, I decided to risk it and hired a few more musicians.

Furthermore, that sombre stage setting simply had to be changed. The little bit of money we'd earned from the first tour we spent on having a white riser built. This time without wheels, mind you! Marjorie and I went in search of elegant, gold-coloured chairs that would go well with the new white riser. We had a good idea of the kind of chairs we wanted, but they appeared to be available only in extremely expensive stores specialising in designer furniture. We couldn't afford them, because all the money at our disposal had already been used up having the riser made. But I've said this before: once I get gold in my head then gold it has to be! After searching for weeks in all the furniture and antique stores in the area we finally found the elegant chairs we were looking for in a sort of 'cash and carry' store in Germany. They cost 27$\frac{1}{2}$ German marks each (about £9.00), with one mark off per chair because we were buying so many.

How happy we were with our new acquisition! The 'gold' was admittedly upholstered with ugly, dark brown corduroy, but we could find a remedy for that. Because of the 'cash and carry' aspect, we had to make several trips back and forth to the store, but at last we got all the chairs home.

Home ... yes, well, it was a bit cramped with fifteen chairs in the living room. It looked as though we were planning a big party, but that was the last thing we had money for at this point. We also had no place to store the riser that had been delivered by truck to our front door. As usual, however, I was lucky, and a friend of mine offered to rent his empty garage to me for a pittance.

As far as the ugly upholstery was concerned, we found a remnant of lovely damask at the market (at least it looked like damask) to re-cover them with. Marjorie cut round pieces out of it and I fastened them to all fifteen chairs with a staple-gun. My 'gold' chairs looked fantastic on stage; no one could tell that we'd covered them with a remnant from the market.

For the ladies in the orchestra I rented colourful evening dresses; The London Strauss Dancers were also asked to appear in more brightly coloured costumes. And lo and behold: the second time around the setting of *Vienna Forever* appeared to have been transformed from a bleak convent into a romantic Viennese *bonbonnière*.

In the years following I kept polishing up and improving my productions and reinvested practically all the money we earned in The Johann Strauss Orchestra, in the firm conviction that one day my concerts would find a much larger public. Each year I added one or two people to the orchestra, and bit by bit I bought everything necessary to perfect my Viennese evenings. I ordered specially made costumes, stage sets, and music stands, bought a very expensive sound system and a second-hand truck, rented a bus for the orchestra and a large shed to store everything in, and hired more personnel. As time went on and we had more and more concerts to play, I could no longer spare the time myself to search for chairs and material to cover them with, no matter how much fun we'd had doing it the first time. In the long run it would also no longer be possible for Marjorie to continue managing the whole administration and organisation by herself.

Between that first tour with The Johann Strauss Orchestra and the 'show' in its present form, there have been years of hard work and struggle: struggling to mould the show into the shape I wanted it to have; struggling for a place on the program at many theatres; struggling against impresarios, producers, and record companies. The hardest part, however, was discovering that there are not only well-meaning people in the world. As a gullible artist with his head in the clouds, I thought for a long time that I could trust everyone I met. Luckily I always had Marjorie, whose background had taught her about the shady practices sometimes found in the business world. She was more cautious than I was in this respect and was almost always able to keep me from believing in the pots of gold at the end of the rainbow that were sometimes promised to me.

In spite of this, the two of us fell into a trap once in a while, and sometimes we really found ourselves in hot water. For weeks we suffered from sleepless nights, afraid that things would never come right again.

Now, many years later, I'm a great deal wiser and can also afford the luxury of surrounding myself with able advisers who have more experience and insight into business affairs than we do. In the early days, though,

The Maastricht Salon Orchestra. From left to right: Jo Huijts (who followed Tjeu Heyltjes as pianist), Marie-Hélène Bertholomé, myself, Frans, and Jean. We're also good friends when we're not working. You automatically share your joys and sorrows with people you work with for so long, and in such a small ensemble it's almost impossible not to become close friends.

The Maastricht Salon Orchestra in 1994. From left to right: the violinist Frans Vermeulen, the double bass player Jean Sassen, myself, the cellist Henriette Janssen, and the pianist Jo Huijts.

Sjef Vink and Willem van Cotthem in Burkina Faso, 1987, planting the trees bought with the proceeds of the Gala Concert.

In 1994, Sjef and Willem proudly inspect the trees that have meanwhile grown to a height of several metres.

The 'Forest of Friendship Maastricht-Niou' in its infancy.

The Johann Strauss Orchestra.

Spring in Vienna, 1991.

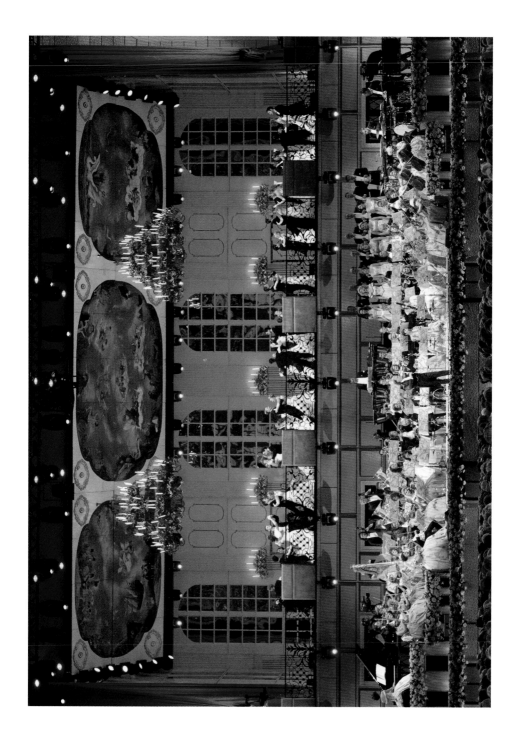

Scenes from productions that took place between 1991 and 1994. Ans Humblet and Ton Hofman in a duet from *Der Zarewitsch (The Tsarevitch)* by Franz Lehár, and 'Là ci darem la mano' from Mozart's *Don Giovanni*.

Melinda Hughes in an aria
from *Das Land des Lächelns*
(The Land of the Smiles)
by Franz Lehár.

Lorenzo Carola and Chris
Waltmans in Figaro's famous
cavatina, 'Largo al factotum',
from *The Barber of Seville*
by Gioacchino Rossini.

The Johann Strauss Orchestra playing its first concert in the famous 'Concertgebouw' in Amsterdam, 1993. The soloists were Tamara Lund and Marco Bakker.

Naturally I've tried to instill a love of the violin in my boys. Although they both have talent, other things interest them more. Pierre plays the piano and is now Vice President of my company. Marc likes to paint, preferably while listening to classical music.

Marc during a performance of *The Ambino Ballet*. He didn't dance, but did a 'playback' to the Serenade by Haydn, played by – who else? – the Maastricht Salon Orchestra.

As young as he was, Pierre could already play a proper scale at this age.

One of my fans once told me that my concerts made her feel as though she was at a children's birthday party: 'cheerful and exuberant, and when it's all over you don't feel at all like going home!' Maybe this is because I like children's birthday parties so much myself, and I try to turn each concert into a truly festive occasion.

'... in his day Johann Strauss often played in the beautiful Viennese Volksgarten, where the people of Vienna came to listen to him. On Sunday, if it was nice weather, they didn't just come to listen to one or two pieces, they sometimes came for the whole day. They would turn it into a special outing, bringing along a blanket to sit on, and a picnic basket with chicken salad and lemonade... and their new girlfriend! And they had a great time. Actually you should try to imagine that you're not really sitting here in this theater, but that you're in Vienna, in the Volksgarten ... sitting on a blanket ... with your chicken salad ...'
During this picnic 'on a blanket' on a sunny day in the middle of winter, our children sang Christmas carols at the top of their voice. It doesn't always have to be Strauss, does it?

We've always been a close family, and we want to keep it that way in spite of our success. I love to do things with my boys and am determined to find time to spend with them.

Every violinist has a picture of a loved one in his violin case. These are the pictures of Marjorie and the boys that I always carry with me. The little boy on the left is Marc, the one on the right, Pierre. Aren't they cute?

things occasionally went wrong. In spite of our caution, sometimes we were really taken for a ride, and each time it happened I was really cut up about it. I just couldn't believe that people did such things on purpose. And that wasn't all: sometimes I was simply too eager to invest. Once I bought some sound equipment, even though I knew that it was

'A big round of applause, ladies and gentlemen, for Ruxandra Voda! She sang an aria from the operetta *Der Vogelhändler (The Bird Seller)* by Carl Zeller.

By the way, Carl Zeller, a contemporary of Johann Strauss, was a very clever man. As a boy he was a member of the Vienna Boys' Choir. Later he studied law and also music, reaching the top in both fields. As a lawyer he rose to become Austria's Minister of Culture, and he was also a respected composer of waltzes and operettas. Well, I guess that's nothing special nowadays. All of our cabinet ministers have jobs on the side, don't they? Some of them even compose, did you know that? Yes, I'm serious! The Dutch Education Minister, Mr Ritzen ... he isn't just a cabinet minister, he's also a composer. Really and truly, he even wrote an operetta recently called *Der Bettelstudent!*' ('*The Beggar Student*' is a famous operetta by Karl Millöcker. Mr Ritzen was responsible for lowering student grants.)

129

much too expensive, just because I wanted the best sound possible. It soon appeared that I'd really gone too far this time. Not only did the bank refuse to lend me any more money, they even sent someone around with an order to sue us for non-payment of our debts. If we remained so overdrawn, they would have the right to confiscate all our earthly possessions, from the office furniture down to the smallest piece of livestock, which in this case meant the poor little zebra finch in my aviary.

This gave me a big shock, but fortunately it never came to that. Probably because I'm a Sunday's child, and I always seem to meet the right people at the right time, and they always help me out of my difficulties.

In this respect I'm very grateful to my bookkeeper, Bob Rutten, a fantastic man with a heart and a voice of gold. He spent practically all of his summer holidays singing in Italy, and he would much rather have become an opera singer than a bookkeeper. Purely out of his love of music, he put heart and soul into my business interests for years, routinely saving me from someone or other's greedy claws. Unfortunately he died a couple of years ago, but in spite of his serious illness, he continued to rejoice in my success till the end of his days, and was glad that my business, thanks in no small part to his own efforts, had managed so well to keep its head above water and ultimately to become the success that it now is.

THE HEADACHES
OF A WIFE
AND MANAGER

A typical example of a try-out and premiere in the early 1990s as seen through the eyes of Marjorie.

'This is your thirty-minute call!' The voice of the stage manager; Pierre Druif resounds over the intercom which can be heard everywhere backstage. For a second the noise dies down; everyone instinctively checks the time.

It's the first try-out of a new program with The Johann Strauss Orchestra, and we're all nervous. I'm probably more nervous than anybody, although unlike the others I won't be required to perform shortly. I don't have to play or sing, I don't have to adjust the lights or sound equipment, all I have to do is watch and listen. That's probably why I'm so nervous. After I've taken my place in the audience, I won't be able to do anything except watch and see if everything runs smoothly. If it doesn't, then all I can do is sit there helplessly, with clammy hands and butterflies in my stomach. My characteristic pessimism tells me that everything is about to go wrong and I won't be able to do anything about it! It's stupid to think this way, I know, because everything has been rehearsed thoroughly and they all know their parts to perfection. Hardly anything ever goes wrong actually. I guess these nerves are just an occupational hazard; after all these years I'm still not able to calm myself down before a concert.

During this final half-hour there's a lot of hustle and bustle in the passageways behind the stage. Musicians are tuning their instruments and trying to warm up. The sounds of winds and strings mingle and clash; the noise is ear-splitting. A violinist complains loudly that she's lost a piece of music, and I help her look for it. Someone else counts out loud while practicing a few dance steps in the hall. I barely manage to avoid being hit by a leg swinging through the air.

---

[16] A vocalise is a singing exercise to warm up the voice using sol-fa syllables or other vowel sounds. They have one harmful side effect, though, and that is that André finds them terribly nerve-racking.

High above everything else, from the singers' dressing rooms come the sounds of vocalises,[16] as well as difficult passages from the arias they'll soon be singing. Stagehands wearing radio headsets hurry back and forth, noisily giving each other last-minute instructions. Somewhere a piece of the set falls over with a crash: better now than during the performance! They quickly set it up again and fasten it more securely. A dress that fit perfectly yesterday now appears to be too big and has to be taken in at the last minute by the seamstress with a couple of 'invisible' safety pins. She talks through the pins between her lips, trying to compensate for lack of clarity by raising her voice.

In the middle of all this commotion is André, silently pacing back and forth, just like he does before every new production: up and down the corridors, back and forth between his dressing room and the stage. He talks to no one. He's concentrating fully on the remarks we've prepared and the anecdotes he's going to tell, repeating to himself the entire program up until the intermission. Back and forth, again and again. I could pick out the sound of his clicking leather soles anywhere.

If you ask me, he walks miles and miles before a try-out! At times like this we all know that we'd better stay out of his way. Talking to him is the last thing you should do. I'm the only one who's still allowed in his dressing room between now and curtain time, but I also keep my mouth closed. I don't want to disturb his concentration.

When the stage manager says 'This is your ten-minute call,' André and the orchestra walk on stage. There is a lot of laughter, which helps to ease the tension. I see one of the orchestra's 'naughty boys' walking around furtively with a roll of Scotch tape and I know what that means. They've made a sport out of taping each other's tails to the chairs before a concert begins, without the victim being aware of it, of course. At some point during the concert, when André motions for the orchestra to stand up, there's always someone whose chair falls over, to the undisguised glee of the perpetrator. When André notices these pranks, he's furious!

Silently I disappear in the direction of the hall. I take my leave with a wink, nothing more, André is definitely not in the mood for small talk. I take care not to say 'good luck' to him or anyone else; in the superstitious world of the theatre this always brings bad luck.

This evening's try-out is not taking place in a theatre. It's a closed affair in the elegant concert hall of a company which has let us rehearse here during weekends for the past few months. As a token of our gratitude we're giving a concert for the employees and their partners.

Luckily I don't have to pass the next couple of nerve-racking hours alone. In the corridor our production manager, Nicole, is already waiting for me, and in the hall I meet my friend Rosy, the dance instructor. She and I taught the steps to the singers who will perform this evening as well as to André. This evening he will dance with a singer for the first time during a performance. (This is probably what I'm most nervous about) Then there is Marian, who is responsible for all the costumes and props. The four of us will watch the performance with a critical eye, because a try-out is not something you do for fun!

We've been doing it like this for a couple of years now. The audience knows that it's witnessing a try-out and is used to seeing us take notes at a table in the back of the hall. Some members of the audience give us a nod of recognition as they come in. A couple of enthusiastic fans come over to tell us that we shouldn't be too severe. André can do nothing wrong in their eyes! I hear a man mumbling something to his wife about 'that poor boy'. I tell Rosy and she bursts out laughing knowing that André is anything but pitiable.

'How are things?' Nicole asks, concerned. I have just enough time to let her know with a sigh and a hand on my stomach that my nerves are acting up terribly, and then the lights in the hall are dimmed. The curtain is raised and the audience whispers 'Ooooh ...!' because the musicians are dressed to the nines. To resounding applause André comes on stage, bows, and strikes up the 'Frühlingsstimmenwalzer' ('Voices of Spring'). I can't tell whether he is still nervous. In any case he doesn't show it, not even I can see any signs of it. Over the years the orchestra has also learned to deal with this tension. The first waltz comes off perfectly, that will give them courage to face the rest of the evening.

Pierre Druif has made an ingenious new set which is subtly reminiscent of a Venetian Doge's palace. In different light it looks more like a bridge, to which use it will be put later on. I've seen it all before, of course, but here on stage in this lovely light it's shown to its best advantage.

Nonetheless I jot down a few things. One of the women is missing a hair clip; there are two women sitting next to each other whose dresses clash. One woman's neck seems a bit bare without a necklace, another's skirt is too short, yet another has a pair of shoes that don't match her dress. I stop writing to listen to André's opening remarks. He's talking to fast. Or I'm thinking too slowly, that's also possible! Either way it's due to tension. Luckily the audience laughs, seeming not to notice anything unusual.

Several instrumental pieces follow, all of which sound charming. The people are obviously enjoying themselves. Then André announces the appearance of the soprano Ans Humblet, who will sing the beautiful aria 'Oh mio babbino caro' ('Oh my beloved Daddy') by Puccini. André gives a short summary of the story. A girl beseeches her father to be allowed to marry her sweetheart. She threatens to jump from the Ponte Vecchio in Florence if her father continues to withhold his consent.

'Ladies and gentlemen, every father's heart will melt at the sound of Ans singing this aria!' I hear a few sniggers from the gentlemen in the hall.

Ans sings this moving aria beautifully, the music seems to have been written for her. After long and heartwarming applause, André asks her to remain on stage. He says that the story she has just sung happened in real life – her own. (The audience laughs; it's obvious they don't believe it.) 'Ans was also not allowed to marry her boyfriend, but when she threatened to jump from the Old Bridge in Maastricht, her father finally gave his permission. And her dear husband is here tonight, none other than our own pianist, Jo Huijts!'

Jo comes forward and folds Ans in his arms. The audience is touched to see the extremely tall Jo and his little Ans, and they applaud enthusiastically. They kiss and for a minute they appear to forget that they're on stage. André calls them back to reality with a loud 'ahem', and they both receive another round of applause.

When André and I were writing this scene we actually stopped to ask ourselves if it would work. We were both afraid that it went a bit too far. Perhaps it was too personal and too romantic, which would cause it to deteriorate into kitsch. It comes over as very sweet and spontaneous, though, and the audience seems to find it wonderful, so that's a load off my mind. I see the others next to me writing and wonder what they think of it.

Except for a couple of minor details, everything runs smoothly. Gradually I manage to calm down, until we reach the finale before the intermission, in which Ans and the tenor Ton Hofman sing and dance the famous duet 'Komm mit nach Varasdin' (Come with me to Varasdin). Rosy and I exchange glances: Oh no! Here it comes! Both of the singers have years of experience singing operetta, they both sing and act wonderfully. Ans also has an incredible talent for dancing, so we're not afraid for her. Ton, on the other hand, had some difficulty learning the steps of this furious foxtrot, which ends with both of them performing a virtuosic cartwheel. After much practice, Ton was able to carry it off during rehearsals, but now I wait anxiously for the end of the dance.

Ans takes a running start for the cartwheel and rotates swiftly and gracefully across the stage. Ton forgets to take a running start, tries to make up for it by taking two clumsy steps, and does a cartwheel that literally never gets off the ground. One leg barely leaves the floor, the other not at all. It seems more like the awkward frolicking of a puppy than a cartwheel. I'm struck speechless, but the audience bursts out laughing. With his radiant laugh and captivating charm, Ton acknowledges the applause as though he's just done a daredevil act on the flying trapeze! The audience likes it so much that I think we'll probably leave it like this.

During the intermission I hurry to André's dressing room to tell him that the program is going very well. Of course he also notices that the concert is a success, but still it's nice to hear it from someone in the audience. We don't talk much, because he wants to rehearse his remarks for the second half, so I just bring him something to drink and then leave him in peace. *The dresser, Annie, stays to help him change. During the second half, André has to change in the wings into a gypsy costume, and he only has forty-five seconds in which to do it, so he puts on part of the costume now underneath his tails.*

The guys in the orchestra are teasing Ton about his 'circus act', but he doesn't mind at all. He enjoyed his acrobatic act more than anyone. He agrees with me that we should let his cartwheel continue to be a flop.

The members of the orchestra assault me with questions: 'How does it sound?' 'Can you hear me all right?' 'In my opinion there's too much bass, did you notice it?' 'Does my dress look all right in that bright light?' 'I played a wrong note somewhere, did you hear it?' I'm able to reassure everyone: it sounds and looks great.

There's no time any more for me to get something to drink. The bell is already ringing for the audience to return to their seats and I hurry along with them.

The third number of the second half is the dreaded gypsy dance, starring André and Ans. When it's time, the butterflies start fluttering again. The orchestra plays a fiery piece of gypsy music, without André, because he's in the wings, changing lightning-quick into his gypsy outfit. Will he be able to do it in just forty-five seconds? My heart skips a beat at the thought... but he did it! He dances onto stage exactly on cue. He looks magnificent in his colourful, shimmering gypsy costume. The dance goes perfectly and the audience applauds wildly. Whew! We certainly worked at it long enough. Relieved, I glance over at Rosy, who sighs just as deeply now that André's debut as a dancer is over.

The rest of the evening doesn't hold anything 'scary' in store for me. At the end of the concert the orchestra plays a potpourri from 'Die Csárdásfürstin' ('The Gypsy Princess') by Emmerich Kálmán. Ans and Ton sing the well-known tunes and waltz without mishap across the stage. The only thing I notice is that once in a while Ton steps on Ans's dress, so we'll have to make it a bit shorter. Luckily there are no cartwheels or other acrobatic tricks in this number!

The audience is now really in the mood and sways back and forth with the music. Here and there people are even singing along softly: 'Tanzen möcht' ich, jauchzen möcht' ich ...' ('I would dance, I would shout for joy').

During the final 'Radetzky March' and the encores, everyone claps along exuberantly. It does me good to see them all enjoying themselves so much, so all those painful and painstaking preparations weren't for nothing. The butterflies in my stomach are finally gone. When the company's director comes on stage to thank André and everyone else who took part, and invites the 'jury' in the back to hold up their score cards, I can laugh along heartily at his joke.

'Once upon a time there was a king and a queen ...'

While leaving the hall I hear the people around me talking enthusiastically about the concert. It's clear that they've had a nice evening because nearly all of them leave talking and laughing gaily, which is wonderful to see. I'm proud of André having done it again, sending his audience home in such high spirits.

Afterwards we have a drink together and give each other a quick summary of our first impressions of this new program. I take the notebooks home which contain the remarks written down by the other three judges. 'I'll study them tonight. I can see that we mostly criticised the same points, so those are things that will definitely have to be changed. Ans and Jo's little romance seems to have been to everyone's liking so that will stay, just like Ton's funny cartwheel.

The next morning at nine o'clock we hold a production meeting to discuss the try-out in detail, after which everyone is told what changes will have to be made this evening. In the afternoon I work a bit on André's script, because some of his anecdotes are too long and others not clear enough. A joke that hardly anyone laughed at is immediately dropped.

This evening there's another try-out in the same hall, two more will take place in theatres elsewhere, and in two weeks is the premiere, on New Year's Day in the theatre in Heerlen. The performance gets better with each try-out and my 'headaches' are proportionately fewer each time. We can look forward to the premiere with confidence.

But it wouldn't be show business if things didn't work out differently than expected. On 30 December Jo phones in the evening to say that Ans is ill and probably won't be able to sing at the premiere. This is highly inconvenient, mostly for Ans of course, but also for us!

I roundly curse all operas and operettas, the man who invented the aria, every singer in the world, and most of all myself, for ever having gotten mixed up in this line of work. If only I were still a teacher! My tirade can't last for long though, because we have work to do, phoning, arranging, organising. Fortunately we have an understudy who can stand in for Ans – Carolina, who has already learned all the pieces in the program. She jumps for joy when she hears that she'll be singing at the premiere. She's seen a few of the try-outs, so she knows about the things that have already been changed, even though there was no time for the orchestra to practice the program with her. That will have to happen tomorrow, on 31 December.

The next day we work for hours in the cold auditorium of a school, the only room this New Year's Eve day that's available to rehearse in. Carolina sings and dances with Ton, with Jo accompanying her on the piano. Rosy and I help her learn the steps, and André conducts. Between the duets and arias we go over the stage directions again and try on the costumes. Working furiously, with pins and needles flying, the seamstress will just about be able to alter them all by this evening. What a nerve-

racking business this is!

By late afternoon everything's been taken care of and we can celebrate New Year's Eve with our children and a few friends. We won't stay up late, because tomorrow we'll need all the energy we can muster.

The relative calm experienced by my insides after the fourth try-out has disappeared completely by now, as I sit in the hall in the theatre in Heerlen on New Year's Day, still tired from yesterday's exertions. There has just been an extra rehearsal for the orchestra, to give them a chance to play through the arias and duets with Carolina. Everything went well, but still.. I'm not happy about it. Our eldest son Marc, who's sitting next to me, says that I should stop worrying.

'It always goes well, Mum, and even if something goes wrong Dad will bullshit his way out of it somehow, just like he always does.'

At times like this it's wonderful to have such an adolescent at your side! Rosy, who's sitting on the other side of me, agrees with Marc completely. Pierre, our youngest son, never sits in the hall, he thinks it's boring. He has André's technical talent and likes the action behind stage, helping with the sets.

The first pieces go well. The audience is very receptive, and that boosts their morale. Shortly before Carolina's first number, André has to tell a story that he found much too long at the try-outs, so we shortened it. He gets the first sentence right, but then – probably because his thoughts are already on Carolina's first aria – he takes a wrong turn, and recites the older, longer version, instead of the newer, shorter one. André has apparently forgotten how the old version went, because the next sentence doesn't follow logically from the one before. Marc looks at me, frowning and says, 'Is it supposed to go like that?' I shake my head and hold my breath. If only this turns out all right! But André, with his wonderful talent for improvisation, has already picked up the thread of the story and happily tells the rest as though nothing had happened.

The rest of the program until the intermission goes smoothly, including the cartwheel number. Carolina is fantastic. No one can tell that she had to stand in for Ans at the last minute. Halfway through the program, when someone has to bring a chair on stage, I see our little Pierre walk on with it. He's dressed in a smart black blazer, with a smug look on his face as though he's had at least ten years of experience as a stagehand. What nerve, he's just like his father!

During the intermission there are 'oliebollen' for everyone,[17] *but I can't even look at them yet. The smell alone is already too much for me. Perhaps I'll eat one later, when it's all over.*

The gypsy dance in the second half is no longer scary for me to watch. It went well in all four try-outs, so it will probably go all right this time. When his forty-five seconds of changing time are up, however, André

[17] A New Year's pastry resembling doughnut holes.

139

doesn't appear! The orchestra plays and Carolina dances by herself across the stage. Rosy, shocked, pinches my arm, because this can't be put right again. A full sixteen bars too late, André finally makes his entry. The dance with Carolina goes beautifully, both of them dancing elegantly around the stage. But then, when the piece has already come to an end, the two of them finish the dance without any music. This is terrible, sixteen bars of dancing in horrifying silence! In reality this takes only a few seconds, but for me it seems an eternity.

Then it's all over, the audiences claps wildly, now that they've seen André dancing for the first time. Did they notice those extra bars or not? Or did they think it was supposed to be like that? I see Rosy wiping the perspiration from her face, so I'm not the only one who had a little anxiety attack at the sight of that mishap. Afterwards André told me that he had managed to change in time, but then, afraid that Carolina wouldn't know when to make her entry, he forgot to come on stage himself!

What is still in store for us? As far as I'm concerned, the rest should now run perfectly, because I've had my share of little upsets for the afternoon. But the worst is yet to come! Carolina sings her last aria – 'Liebe, du Himmel auf Erden' ('Love live forever') – in a strapless gold dress. I'm not fond of strapless dresses anyway, but after today my antipathy knows no bounds. Before Carolina has even finished her first line, I notice that the bodice of her dress has started to slip down. Rosy has seen it too, and at the same time we both instinctively clutch at the necklines of our own dresses. That dress couldn't possibly ... No, it's impossible, I can't bear to think about it! With each breath she takes (and that's quite a few in an aria like this), the dress slips down a bit more. By now I no longer dare to look, and keep my gaze riveted on my knees. If only she'd finish. But no, she still has a whole couplet to go. I hear Marc next to me, sniggering. What on earth is happening?

At last the aria is over. I hear applause and, with my eyes still closed, I quietly ask Rosy, 'Does she still have it on?'

'Sure, just look and see,' and only then do I dare look at Carolina. Apparently nothing has happened. While bowing she manages to pull her dress up into place with a skillful, almost invisible movement of her hand, before skipping merrily into the wings.

I have the greatest admiration for her, as well as for André and Ton and all the others who always go on with the show, no matter what happens on stage. I certainly couldn't do it! I'd rather sit in the audience, with butterflies in my stomach.

At the end of the concert the mood in the Heerlen theatre is distinctly festive. The people are wildly enthusiastic, balloons and streamers fill the air, there are lots of flowers for the performers, and a standing ovation. André gives several encores, they obviously don't want him to leave. Then the curtain falls and I go to the artists lounge. Lots of people come backstage to tell André how much they loved the concert. They shower praise on him and the soloists, and congratulate everyone on the brilliant premiere.

Still shaking from having lived through such anxious moments, I tell an acquaintance how I died a thousand deaths in the course of the afternoon.

'You did? Why? Did something go wrong?'

Rosy gives me a sympathetic look. 'Come on,' she says, and pulls me along by my sleeve. Together we walk in the direction of the 'oliebollen' and champagne. We think we deserve some.

AT LAST!

*S*ince 1978 I'd been investing in my own ensembles. By now it will be clear to all my readers that in the years described so far my family was not living in the lap of luxury. I had been told that seven 'lean' years were always followed by seven 'fat' ones, so I'd been expecting them to start since about 1985. I'm not sure why – perhaps because I do everything so thoroughly and would rather do something twice than do it by halves – in any case, it took another seven years before the scales began to tip the other way. Only then could we begin, very cautiously, to pluck the fruits of our labour, and, in my opinion, it was high time we did!

For years we had worked hard to turn our Viennese evening into a truly professional performance, and in this we'd succeeded. More and more theatre managers in the Netherlands and Belgium were enthusiastic about our show and offered engagements to The Johann Strauss Orchestra. The concert-goers had grown to know and love us, and the halls we played in were invariably filled to the last seat. Usually our concerts were already sold out at the beginning of the year, all of the places being taken by holders of season tickets. Many of the people who had been to one of our concerts wrote to me to let me know how much they'd enjoyed the evening.

All in all, I had been led to believe that it must be possible to bring our music to a much wider public, and not just to those who came to the theatres where we returned every year. I was thinking of a public far beyond the borders of the Benelux, and the best way to achieve this goal was naturally television.

Together Marjorie and I launched an extensive campaign to conquer this medium. Just as, once upon a time, we had tried to sell The Maastricht Salon Orchestra to theatres and radio stations, we began once again to peddle our wares, both the salon orchestra (I thought that the Hieringebiete Concert and the 'Speculaas' Concert were very telegenic) and The Johann Strauss Orchestra. In the meantime we'd had a lot more experience, so the whole process would be much easier. Or so we thought. We telephoned, wrote letters, and sent tapes, photographs, and videos. We got in the car and drove to Hilversum regularly to talk personally with producers, program makers, and presenters.

The results were depressing. 'Hilversum' thought I was crazy. The classical music department didn't think my music was serious enough, the producers of pop music just burst out laughing and told me to go play for my grandmother. Almost all of them found the music of both The Maastricht Salon Orchestra and The Johann Strauss Orchestra corny and old-fashioned. Who on earth would play such stuff and what kind of crazy audience would want to listen to it? The few who did see something in it were either just about to be pensioned off, in the process of moving abroad, coming down with a serious illness, or, even worse, about to die before they could help us. Luck didn't seem to be on our side.

Maybe it would be better to hire an impresario who had connections with people in television. We went in search of a suitable candidate, but continued to run into people who either tried to defraud us or else thought they could keep us dangling forever, until our patience ran out. We tried the same tactics in other countries. We phoned large agencies in Paris and Berlin, and travelled to Brussels, Hannover, and Munich to try our luck there, but everywhere we heard the same old tune: 'You've got a cute act, but there's no public for it. In this day and age you really can't put such stuff on TV anymore.'

If Marjorie and I hadn't been so persevering –
all the time feeling intuitively that everyone was mistaken,
that there really was a very large public indeed for my music –
then there would have been plenty of times when we were
both ready to throw in the towel.
It was all extremely exhausting, and once in a while
we really got fed up with constantly searching for
yet more contacts and forever repeating the same old story.
Still, we both remained firmly convinced that it was precisely
'in this day and age' – in these modern, hectic times,
in which so many people lead stressful lives –
that lots of people yearn for the romanticism of the
good old days, for a touch of nostalgia, and especially
for relaxed and sociable evening entertainment.

We gradually realised that we had to try a different tack or we would never succeed in getting a concert on television. What we really needed was a record of our Viennese evening and a large record company that was willing to promote us. With renewed enthusiasm – the same energy and inspiration I had shown as a child when I was planning an addition to 'the Cart', and later on with each new step in my career – I took to the war path. This time I tried hawking my wares at record companies. This simply had to produce results! If only I could persuade a record company executive to come to one of our concerts, he couldn't help but be convinced of the quality of our work and offer me a contract ...

I don't want to bore my readers by constantly repeating myself, but I'll have to if I want to tell the story as it really happened. History repeated itself, and again I was rejected all along the line. 'Not interested', 'Nothing special', 'Can't sell it', 'Only interesting for the elderly, and they don't buy records', 'Nice concert, but nothing for a record', and so on. The many record companies that rejected me in those days will undoubtedly remember their comments. (And now, inasmuch as a company can do it, they're being forced to eat their words!)

My odyssey through Record Land ended in Hilversum, at Phonogram, where product manager Herman van der Zwam, after attending one of my concerts, said immediately, 'This is it! We're going to make a record with this man!'

That record, or rather CD, came out. At last. In August 1994 a single was issued with the *Waltz No. 2* from *Jazz Suite No. 2* by Shostakovich, better known as *The Second Waltz*, followed a month later by the album *Strauss & Co. (From Holland With Love)*. The record company hoped to sell 25,000 by the end of the year.

From the moment the single came out, one surprise followed another. *The Second Waltz* conquered Holland practically overnight. It climbed to the Dutch Tip Parade and then the Hit Parade, and before long it was even in the Top Ten, where it stayed for months. It was unbelievable, a moving, magnificent concert waltz, a purely classical piece by Dmitri Shostakovich, there in the Top Ten among all the pop groups!

During a live radio interview with the famous Dutch disc jockey Frits Spits, I had to announce the *Radetzky March* from the album *From Holland With Love*, and I used the slogan that my son Marc had thought up for me: 'Not house, but Strauss!' This motto was responsible for conquering, in no time, Radio 3 (the pop station) and with it the youth of the Netherlands. The album was released in the Top Hundred, quickly climbed to first place, and stayed there for a long time. For fifty-two continuous weeks it stayed in the Top Ten, a record never before attained in the Netherlands.

Two months after the album was released another exciting event took place. On 18 November 1994 our first television concert was broadcast in the Netherlands: *From Holland With Love*, which had been recorded at the concert hall 'De Vereniging' in Nijmegen. (This concert has often been broadcast on PBS as well.) We were dying to see what would happen. Would my prediction come true? Would my concert be as successful as I expected it to be? Or were all those pessimists right in thinking that 'except for a few theatre-goers' there was no public for my music?

The morning after the broadcast I received a phone call from the producer, Marjolein Mulder. Excited and with a voice that kept breaking from emotion, she told me that my concert had been given an incredibly high rating, the highest since the European soccer championships, which the Dutch had won. The only other person who ever got such a high rating had been Wim Kan with his famous political cabaret on New Year's Eve.

With tears in our eyes Marjorie and I fell into each other's arms. At first we could hardly believe it. Had so many people really watched my concert, and had it really been given such a high rating? We were beside ourselves with joy and immediately went to the office to spread the good news. Within minutes everyone was jubilant. We put on *The Second Waltz*, which was on the phone for people on hold, and turned up the sound as loud as possible. To the crackling sound that came out of all the telephones simultaneously, everyone danced around the office, exuberant and elated.

How happy we were! Not only Marjorie and I, but also the orchestra and all our staff. This had surpassed everyone's expectations. It was the best possible reward anyone could have given us for all those years of hard work.

The television broadcast unleashed a whole chain of reactions. So many people started to phone up to book us for concerts that very soon we couldn't handle the requests any longer ourselves, and put the responsibility for bookings into the experienced hands of Wout van Liempt of the Nederlands Theatrebureau. Before the end of 1994, the sales figures for *From Holland With Love* had far surpassed the expected 25,000 to reach an incredible 250,000, and this has meanwhile risen to 800,000, a figure that has never before been reached in the Netherlands in such a short time! The following record, *Wiener Mélange (The Vienna I Love)*, as well as the videos clips that appeared, were also sold in record numbers.

Suddenly I was showered with attention. I won prizes and was decorated with honours, flowers and chocolates were named after me, and I had to give dozens of interviews for the press, the radio, and television. Many hosts of television shows invited me to appear on their program – alone or with The Johann Strauss Orchestra – and I received offers to make commercials and was invited to participate in other advertising campaigns. I'd become a star overnight, enjoying the benefits as well as suffering the consequences. What has happened to me since *The Second Waltz* has been so well documented by both the serious and less serious magazines and papers that I don't have much more to add to it.

All this has changed our lives overnight. It's as though events have accelerated out of control and we often have to stop and take stock of the situation to make sure we still have both feet firmly on the ground. I'm overjoyed at the success we both worked toward for so long, though I try to keep a cool head about it. I work in the same way and with the same enthusiasm I used to. I don't intend to give up my fighting spirit either, because I know that whatever I undertake, I'll always run up against obstacles, and there will always be skeptics I'll have to win over to my side. But it's all worth it in the end, because there's nothing more fantastic than making music with wonderful colleagues for an appreciative audience!

My boyhood dreams have come true, the one about the angel already thirty-eight years ago, and in 1994 that other dream too, the dream of the little boy who wanted so much to stand in the spotlight and play the violin for lots and lots of people. I'm truly a happy man!

PART FOUR

*M*r RIEU,
MAY I ASK YOU A QUESTION?

MAY I ASK YOU
A QUESTION?

*A*fter playing an agreeable Sunday morning concert with The Maastricht Salon Orchestra a lady came up to me. She spoke to me, slightly embarrassed. 'Mr Rieu, may I ask you a personal question?'

The lady's age, which in spite of her dark wig I estimated to be at least eighty, led me to assume that it wouldn't be at all dangerous to answer in the affirmative, so I said, 'Yes.'

'Would you play at my funeral?'

I almost choked on my coffee, took out my engagement book, and, somewhat shocked, said, 'Okay, just tell me when.'

Ever since then I've seen the lady in question every year at one of my concerts. She still wears her dark wig and seems to be in the best of health. Apparently she prefers to listen to me 'live', and I hope this will keep her going for quite some time.

In spite of the joke I made about it, it does touch me to be asked such a question. After all, dying, taking leave of loved ones and everything surrounding the mourning process, is a terrifying thought for most of us. When people in such a situation say they find solace in my music, I take it as a huge compliment, and as yet more evidence that music in general – it doesn't matter what kind; after all, tastes differ – is capable of touching people to the quick. As long as I succeed in doing this with my concerts, I know that what I do is good, and that I have an important mission to fulfill.

(Just so I'm not inundated with requests to play at funerals, let me say right away that I find it so dreadful that I practically never do it. It only takes one note on the violin to make the people assembled in the church or funeral home start weeping so pitifully that I can't go on playing. Then I start crying even louder than all the next of kin put together and am certainly not worth my fee at such moments.)

Someone phones the office and gets a receptionist on the line who has just been hired that morning and is answering her first telephone call.

'Good morning, Miss, I'm making a statue of Mr Rieu, but in photographs I can only see the top half of him. Could you please give me the measurements of his bottom half?'

Receptionist: 'I beg your pardon! What on earth ...? What kind of place is this?'

A question often asked in letters: 'Mr Rieu, what is the colour scheme in your living room? I'm drawing/painting/knitting/crocheting/sewing/embroidering/needlepointing a portrait of you which I'd like to frame and give to you, and it would be nice if it matched your décor.'

My dear public, I think it's fantastic that so many of you want to do this for me, and I admire your resourcefulness and creativity in finding new ways to make portraits of me. But where on earth am I supposed to put them all? You couldn't even see the original colours in my living room if I filled it with all the presents I'm swamped with daily. I really appreciate the fact that you take so much trouble to make me something in order to express your gratitude for the music I give you, but I think I have a better suggestion. You know that my heart goes out to the people in Burkina Faso and that I'd like to do everything I can to help them. You could do me no greater favour than supporting me in this effort. It would be wonderful if, instead of sending me presents, you would make a donation to the Committee Maastricht-Niou. Every ten guilders (£3) means another tree in the Sahel region. This would make me happy indeed, and of course the people in that poor African country would be happier still! I would be very grateful to you.

'Would you like to play for the King and the Queen?'

'Of course I would. But I would like it best of all if they bought a ticket for one of my concerts! Not because I'm greedy, you understand. I love to play, for anyone and everyone, but preferably for people who come to listen because they want to. The most enthusiastic members of the audience are those who have had to wait in line a long time to buy a ticket. These contrast starkly with those poor souls who got free tickets from some company or other, either because they work there or because they're good customers. They never know what to expect at such a concert. Maybe they only like Renaissance music, or their favourite performer is Nana Mouskouri. Such evenings are never the success they might have been, because the audience is served music that it didn't order.

And I wouldn't think of doing that for the world, imposing my music on the King and the Queen!

♫ ♪ ♫

A snobbish male voice on the line: 'Hello, you're speaking with Dr N. Would your husband be so kind as to play with his little orchestra at my wife's birthday get-together next Saturday evening? Of course I'd be willing to pay him for playing.'

Answer: 'Unfortunately my husband has a previous engagement that evening. But now that I have you on the line... his appendix has been giving him trouble lately. Would you be so kind as to remove it for him? Of course he'd be willing to pay you for doing it!'

♫ ♪ ♫

'Mrs Rieu, does Mr Rieu also play at the better sort of weddings?'
Unfortunately he had a previous engagement that evening as well.

♫ ♪ ♫

A question I positively hate: 'Oh, André, I'd like it so much if you could come to my birthday party. It's next week, on Friday, can you make it?'

'Gosh, it's nice of you to invite me. Yeah, sure, I even seem to be free that evening. I'd really like to come!'

'Great, will you bring your violin along?'

Aaaargh....

Marjorie found a note on her desk asking her to return a call to a company that was interested in booking a concert. A very nice woman answered, who proceeded to ask her dozens of questions about me. Marjorie is used to this and answered her questions courteously. After all, the customer is always right.

After about ten minutes of this the woman suddenly said, 'I really must tell you the truth, Mrs. Rieu. You're talking to the wrong person. This is the Institute for War Invalids. I knew right away that you'd dialed the wrong number, but I love your husband's music so much that I didn't have the heart to tell you!'

♫ ♪ ♫

Pianist Wanted

One day a man came to audition for us who said in a sad voice that he thought he would be an eligible candidate for The Maastricht Salon Orchestra. He looked so sad that I thought he was going to burst into tears any minute. He sat down at the piano and began to play a difficult fugue by Bach, whereby his face took on an even sadder appearance. I thought of *Susie* and asked gently if he was really at the right address.

'Yes.'

That was all.

I wanted to cheer him up a bit, and asked brightly, 'Would you like a cup of coffee?'

'No.'

'Or would you rather have tea?'

'No.'

Again he started to play Bach, a different fugue this time. When I asked if he also played Mozart, he gave me a withering look. He didn't mind playing a melancholy nocturne by Chopin, but when that was over he seemed closer to crying than laughing. Me too, in fact. The atmosphere was getting darker by the minute. I tried again. 'Could I offer you some other refreshment?'

'No, thank you. No coffee, no tea, no wine, no women. None of that in my life,' said the man, suddenly very determined and persuasive. The effort of sticking to his principles caused a wrinkle to form above his nose. I really felt sorry for him.

That same day Jo Huijts came to audition. He played like a god: Mozart, Chopin, and Beethoven, and after all that he even played *Susie* with me. First he drank coffee, then tea, then he ate two pieces of pie. He sat there chatting away for hours. Sitting next to my wife on the sofa,

154

Always a great pleasure: working with Frank Steijns to compose new pieces for The Johann Strauss Orchestra. We both enjoy this enormously.

he happily drank one glass of white wine after the other, and when that was finished, he started on red.

He was the one I hired. You can't blame me, I'm only human!

♪ ♫ ♪

From an interview for a school newspaper:

'Have you ever made a big blunder during a concert? If so, what was it?'
'I forgot to take along my violin!'
'How did you get into the orchestra you're playing with now?'
'Ha, ha, that's a good one.'

The questions most often asked by children:

Do you play any other instruments beside the violin?

Yes, piano, but not very well. When I play, I like best to improvise, trying to compose new melodies. For many years I also played the recorder, which I really liked. But now I'm glad that I play the violin.

What are your hobbies?

I love animals. As a child I had two dogs, a parrot, a pigeon, fish, lizards, salamanders, frogs, and even a snake. Now I have two dogs, an aviary full of birds, and a fish pond. For a while we also had chickens and guinea pigs.

Another favourite hobby of mine is technology. I like to watch TV programs about modern technology and new discoveries in all kinds of fields. For me one of the most interesting things is space travel, though I wouldn't like to be an astronaut myself. But I would like to be a pilot, and I've even had a couple of flying lessons.

*W*hat is your favourite food?

I don't know. I like everything. I'm crazy about oysters, which I eat every year at the Preuvenemint in Maastricht.[18] On the other hand, I also like mashed potatoes with raw chicory and red onions and krèpkes (Maastricht dialect for crisp pieces of bacon). But only if Marjorie makes it.

*W*ho is your favourite composer?

Again such a difficult question! I love all kinds of music, if it's well-composed and performed with real feeling. But if I have to name a few favourites, then I would have to say Johann Strauss (naturally), Mozart, and Verdi.

*W*hat is your favourite television program?

I like best to watch tennis matches, often late at night after returning from a concert. I'm not really for anyone in particular, simply for the one playing the best at that moment. A young upstart beating an established star is especially fun to watch. Otherwise I like comedies, such as *Allô, allô* and *Fawlty Towers*. I don't watch them if I'm by myself, but together with Marjorie and the boys I laugh my head off at those programs.

*A*ndré, would you please come play at my First Communion?

(This question has a 'grown-up' variation: 'Would you please play at my wedding?')

I'd really like to, but if I play at your Communion (wedding), then

---

[18] This is a culinary event that takes place every summer in Maastricht's main square.

I also have to play at your neighbour's, otherwise it wouldn't be fair, would it? And there are so many First Communions and weddings, I wouldn't have time for anything else. So just celebrate without me, and put on a record with music by Johann Strauss. That will put everyone in a festive mood!

Questions most often asked by adults:

*W*hy did you leave the symphony orchestra?

As a result of the unique atmosphere during concerts with The Maastricht Salon Orchestra and The Johann Strauss Orchestra, I began to feel more and more dissatisfied when I had to play in the symphony. Although I love classical music, and I found most of our repertoire interesting, the atmosphere at those symphony concerts began to get on my nerves. The orchestra sat on stage playing the most beautiful music, the audience sat in the hall listening attentively, but I didn't feel any emotional exchange between the two groups. Of course I don't mean to say that people can't enjoy classical music tremendously. But there's hardly any way for them to express it except by applauding with varying degrees of enthusiasm when the piece is finished. It's also difficult to sense any emotion flowing from the musicians toward the audience. They watch the conductor and do their best to play well and not to make any mistakes. What kind of people are sitting in the audience and what they think of the concert doesn't really interest them, though. The musicians are playing more for the sake of the music at that point and not specifically for the audience in the hall, which is something we certainly are doing with The Maastricht Salon Orchestra and The Johann Strauss Orchestra.

Such things began to irritate me more and more, and I began to yearn for a life as an independent musician, and the possibility to make music the way I wanted to. I also remembered what my father always used to say to me, 'You should make sure that you have a specialty in life, you should concentrate on doing one thing and do it really well.'

Eventually this led to my saying farewell to the symphony orchestra after playing in it for twelve years, resulting in the loss of all the security offered by a permanent job. Naturally I didn't take this step without talking things over thoroughly with Marjorie. We were both convinced that it was a risk we just had to take, and to this day I've never regretted it.

You receive a good deal of criticism from classical music circles. Do you mind?

Naturally I'm annoyed at this, because I find it unjustified. There are some things you just can't compare. The only thing I do is to smooth the way for many people who have always felt a barrier between themselves and classical music. Classical music lovers should actually be grateful for this. It's a real pity that classical music is shrouded in earnestness and elitism, and I intend to keep fighting to change this. A great deal of classical music is worthy of being brought to a much wider public.

After a concert with The Maastricht Salon Orchestra, an elderly man came up to me and said, 'I'd never seen or heard a violin from close up until now, and I think it makes a lovely sound.' Thanks to our concert, people like him might then go to hear a violin concert by Bruch or Beethoven, and they might like that too. Isn't that fantastic?

Why shouldn't you be allowed to make it easier for people to listen to classical music? Many people feel ill at ease at the idea of going to a concert. They aren't used to listening to classical music, and they're uncomfortable with the tradition of long black dresses and tails, the serious faces, the sombre setting, and the stiff, stately atmosphere that permeates the hall. Classical music simply has an elitist image: 'That's nothing for people like us!' I've heard this said so many times. But there's so much wonderful music that many more people would be able to enjoy, if only it were presented to them in the right way. Just look at what happened to 'my' Shostakovich waltz!

Naturally there are now lots of people who can sing *The Second Waltz*, but don't know that it's by Shostakovich and don't know the correct title or opus number (as real lovers of classical music supposedly should!). But what's so bad about that? Before the Dutch flautist Berdien Stenberg became known for her Rondo Russo, I'd never heard of the composer Mercadante, and I still don't know the opus number – I'm not good at remembering opus numbers anyway – but I think it's a marvellous piece, and I'm convinced that it's caused a lot of people to sit up and listen to classical music. And that's the most important thing, being able to enjoy music.

I play *The Second Waltz* in its original form, I haven't changed it at all, haven't added a popular 'beat' to it or anything. The only thing I do is play it with a great deal of pleasure, and I make this clear to the audience. And it's not just me, my whole orchestra exudes this feeling.

That solemn atmosphere that people associate with classical music in the concert hall, which frightens away a wider public, is not to be found at our concerts. I talk a bit, make a few jokes – never at the expense of the music, though – and put the audience at ease. After the first piece and my first 'speech', I see the tension disappearing from their faces and an atmosphere is created in which you can see the people thinking: well, well, this is fun, I hope it goes on like this the whole evening. And in such a relaxed atmosphere it goes without saying that it's also fun for us to play, night after night after night. You can tell that you're making the audience happy with music, and what more could a musician wish for?

It's no coincidence that people cough so much between movements at concerts of classical music! Those people can't all have colds, they're just nervous because they're practically holding their breath while the orchestra is playing, afraid to move for fear of annoying their neighbours. No one ever coughs at our concerts, at least not from nervousness. If someone with a cold does start coughing uncontrollably, I simply offer him a cough drop, and go on with the concert.

Luckily I also receive my share of compliments from the 'classical corner'. The biggest compliment came from Riccardo Chailly and the Concertgebouw Orchestra in Amsterdam. After conducting a Mahler symphony, Chailly – with a broad smile on his face – made them play *The Second Waltz* as an encore. And the whole audience, who had come to hear Mahler, started swaying back and forth to the sound of Shostakovich!

W̶hat do you hate?

Snobs!

A columnist for the *NRC Handelsblad* asked herself jokingly if the members of my orchestra were chosen on the basis of sex, because the ladies in their splendid dresses all sit at the front, and the men in tails at the back.

This is certainly not the case (of course not!), although you would think so if you saw The Johann Strauss Orchestra on television. The only criteria are being able to play well and enjoying the kind of music I play. The positions of the various groups of instruments on stage – the strings in front and the winds in back – is the traditional one and has to do with the intensity of the sound they make. The members of The Johann Strauss Orchestra rotate, meaning that the make-up of the various groups often changes, so it can easily happen that at some concerts almost all of the strings are women. There are quite a few male string players, though, especially in the violin section. On the other hand, most of the brass and percussion players are men. There are always exceptions to the rule, however, as witnessed by our one female percussion player.

♫ ♪ ♫

I'm often asked during interviews about my worst quality. I can't judge this myself, of course, but according to Marjorie there is one that is high on the list: I'm a real pig!

When Marjorie came to visit me for the first time in my garret in Brussels, she discovered not only that I was an attentive lover, but also that she would certainly never be bored as long as she was with me. There was work to be done! My room was a real pigsty and she couldn't stand it. In my refrigerator she found jars with more mould than apple-sauce, rancid butter, meat that had gone off, decomposing vegetables, milk that was months old, vinegary wine, and other appetizing things. I knew it, of course, but I couldn't have cared less. The refrigerator smelled horrible, so I no longer opened it. My mother had abandoned all attempts years ago to teach me to be clean and tidy, because I seemed to be beyond help.

Once, when I was still very little, my mother, who was in the kitchen, noticed that a lot of people had congregated on the sidewalk in front of our living room window and were staring inside, greatly amused. She went to have a look for herself and found me standing on the window-sill. I'd taken off my nappy and was happily smearing its contents all over the window!

When my brother Robert and I were in high school, we developed the habit of eating an orange in bed before falling asleep at night. We threw the peels in a wastebasket that we then pushed under the bed as far as we could. The children in our family were responsible for order and cleanliness in their own rooms, and we didn't see anything in ours to worry about. Then one day our mother stopped dead in her tracks outside our door because of the pungent smell that was coming from our room. After searching for a while she found the stinking wastebasket with a couple of fresh orange peels on top. When she turned it upside down, the mouldy orange peels underneath, pressed into a stiff mass, stayed standing in the shape of the basket. My mother was furious. I didn't un-derstand why, because I was fascinated by the unique shape and beauti-ful colours of that mouldy mass!

I'm not as bad as I used to be, though. (For one thing, I no longer get the chance!) But I'm still convinced that there are much more important things in the world than being clean and tidy. (Yuck!)

*W*hat do you think of music critics?

I think I'm probably no different from most other artists. I recently read the answer that the film director Marleen Gorris gave to the same question: 'Sometimes a pain in the a-.' Someone who's just received an Oscar can say that in public, but I can't.

Actually I feel sorry for them, those ladies and gentlemen who earn their living as critics. You should try sitting there in the concert hall, night after night, always knowing everything better but not being allowed to do it! Once I felt so sorry for the critics attending a concert given by The Maastricht Salon Orchestra that I asked two of them to come on stage and invited them to play along with us. (I respected these critics' opinion because when they wrote about me they always judged me on my own merits, within the framework of the sort of music I play.)

Both critics were given an instrument to hold, one of them a whip and the other copper bells. I put the music of the *St Petersburg Sleigh Ride* in front of them and asked if they could read music. If not, then all they had to do was try to follow the rhythm as best they could, the important thing was coming in on time. Both of them had a lot of fun and played for all they were worth, to the great delight of the audience. After crossing the finish line together, they bowed, graciously acknowledging the applause they received for their performance, and took their seats again.

But I wasn't through teasing them yet, and so I pulled a newspaper article out of the inside pocket of my tails.

'Ladies and gentlemen, as usual, the review of this concert was already written last night, because the critics have to go to a party after this, so I'll go ahead and read you an item from tomorrow's paper.

'... The melodies were nevertheless executed with an innate musicality, every facet of which was sublimely rendered down to the last particular, without however unjustly neglecting the compositorial underpinnings, and, moreover, with extreme dedication and painstaking attention to detail, causing complete infiltration of the harmonious tonality, the total equilibrium of which was thereby shown to advantage.'

The audience had a good laugh at this, but the two critics – good sports, both of them – laughed harder than anyone. Neither one had any difficulty recognising a bit of his own style in this nonsense!

THE SHOW
MUST GO ON

I'm often asked, both in interviews and by fans, what I find most annoying about my profession.

I always find this question extremely difficult. I think I have a wonderful profession, perhaps the best that exists. When someone asks me a question like that, I hardly know what to answer. Of course it has its tiresome aspects, just like any job. And certainly if you run your own business you'll have to do things that no one finds fun, such as firing people. I always find this very difficult, but I guess I'm no different from most employers in this respect. Sometimes you can't avoid such things, and then you just have to grin and bear it.

I also hate it when things don't go according to plan, when people don't keep to their contracts or agreements, when equipment breaks down at the wrong moment – computers, printers, sound systems, you name it. But these are all problems encountered in any job, and everyone finds them annoying.

One thing that holds true especially in this profession – not just for me but for all artists – is the famous saying 'The show must go on'. Once you're standing on stage, facing hundreds or even thousands of people who are really looking forward to your concert, then you have to perform to perfection. No complaining, no matter how awful you feel, even if you're in pain or extremely distressed about something. The audience expects you to give your concert as though nothing were wrong. This can be far from pleasant, but it's part of the job and I've grown used to it. It's something I picked up at home at a very early age. I saw my father as well as other artists, often great soloists, lying in bed with a burning fever a couple of hours before a concert, only to get up and perform, pepped up with the necessary remedies. Full of admiration for so much perseverance, I once witnessed a fantastic concert given by Herman Krebbers, whom I'd seen on his last legs at our house only a short while before the concert. That night he played more brilliantly than ever!

A short while ago I ran into the principal of the elementary school our children attended when they were small. He congratulated me on my current success, and told me that the school was very proud to have been the venue for the first rehearsals of The Johann Strauss Orchestra. He thought it was fantastic, all that had happened since. He went on to say, however, that even though he's an enthusiastic amateur musician, he wouldn't want to trade places with me for all the money in the world.

'André, do you know what impressed me the most? That you jumped in the car and raced off to give a concert that day Pierre fell at school. I would never have been able to do that.'

I knew immediately what he was talking about. It happened several years ago, on a sunny, spring day, just when I was about to leave for Louvain, near Brussels, where I had a concert that evening. I was sitting in the garden with Marjorie and was just about to say goodbye, when suddenly one of our staff came running toward us. The garden was supposed to be strictly private and normally personnel were forbidden to set foot there. So we knew that something awful must have happened. Someone had phoned from school, she said, breathless with fright, we had to go over there right away, Pierre had fallen from the jungle gym!

What a disaster! We jumped into the car and raced off in the direction of the school, not knowing whether we'd find him dead or alive. School was just out, so dozens of children were crowded around our son, who lay on the ground, deathly pale. Luckily we could see at once that he was still alive, though he lay there groaning from the pain.

Everything was in chaos. Pierre's worried teacher was kneeling beside him, looking even paler than Pierre. The principal had gone to phone a doctor, a female colleague was trying to calm down the other children in Pierre's class, and someone else was trying to send the rest of the school home.

The doctor arrived, made a preliminary diagnosis of a broken leg and perhaps a concussion, and said that Pierre should be taken to the hospital. We weren't allowed to take him ourselves, so I called an ambulance from the car phone. Marjorie rode along in the ambulance, and I drove to the hospital in my own car, because somewhere at the back of my mind I knew that I had to play a concert that evening. In the meantime, though, I didn't have time to give it any more thought, Pierre being the subject of my immediate concern.

Luckily things turned out better than expected, his leg and a couple of ribs were bruised, not broken, and he didn't have a concussion after all. Not until I was sure of this and had seen the x-rays myself did I dare to jump in the car and drive to Louvain at breakneck speed, arriving just in time for the concert.

That night we gave a marvellous concert, and I'm sure the audience didn't notice anything, even though the fright I'd just had stayed with me for hours. The worst part was not being able to stay with little Pierre that evening. At such moments I could curse my profession!

Once he'd gotten over the initial shock and recovered from the pain, Pierre himself was able to joke about the whole thing. Afterwards he even told us that when he was lying there half-conscious on the ground he'd heard his teacher ask one of his classmates how it had happened. 'Well,' answered the boy, 'Pierre hanged on the jungle gym, and then suddenly he fell.'

'Hung!' corrected the teacher, in spite of the panic all around him. And that's how it should be. 'The show must go on', also for teachers!

One last question:

*W*hat is your dearest wish?

That I may go on making people happy with my music for many years to come!